97 Powerful Safety Tips for Women

for Women

How to Protect Your Loved Ones in Dangerous Times

by

Damian Brindle

97 Powerful Safety Tips for Women: How to Protect Your Loved Ones in Dangerous Times by Damian Brindle

Published by Great Books, LLC

P.O. Box 1157

Liberty, MO. 64069

Visit the author's website at https://rethinksurvival.com

ISBN: 9798695075458 (print)

Printed in U.S.A.

First Edition

Disclaimer

Every effort has been made by the author and publishing house to ensure that the information contained in this book was correct as of press time. The author and publishing house hereby disclaim and do not assume liability for any injury, loss, damage, or disruption caused by errors or omissions, regardless of whether any errors or omissions result from negligence, accident, or any other cause. Readers are encouraged to verify any information contained in this book prior to taking any action on the information.

Table of Contents

Introduction

This book is intended to provide useful, actionable safety strategies as quickly as possible. As such, it's written to be fast to read and includes minimal images. Links are provided to referenced materials and products should you want additional information or to purchase the product.

How This Book is Organized

Overall, the book is organized into major locations of concern including being at home, walking around the neighborhood, while out shopping, and so on. Each location of concern includes several to dozens of effective strategies I recommend you take. That said, some actions are focused on more so than others, as such they may require a page or two to discuss. All other actions should be relatively self-explanatory and only need a paragraph or two to explain.

But You're a Man! You Can't Possibly Understand What's It's Like Being a Woman

Yes, that's true. I've been told as much when deciding to write this book. And while I don't pretend to understand what it must be like, I do have an affinity for my personal safety along with a strong desire to keep the women in my own life safe from harm, at least as much as I reasonably can. I figure that if I can help you or a loved stay safe in the process then I'm happy to share what I know. Realize, too, that this book was a collaborative process as many other good folks just like you shared with me their own tips to make the book even better. Thank you all.

About Website Links

Understand that this book was originally written to be an electronic book only with many website links referenced throughout. Because this is a paperback book, however, referencing these links can be tedious if you had to type them into your web browser by hand. To make this easier on you, I have consolidated all referenced links into one page here: https://rethinksurvival.com/books/safety-links.html.

When new links are introduced, they will be referenced with superscripts which will then correspond to the appropriate URL on the above referenced website page.

For completeness, all referenced links will also be included in Appendix C.

Grab Your Free 97-Point Checklist

Odds are that you won't remember everything discussed when you're done reading this book. To make your life easier I've created a free, easy-to-reference 97-point safety checklist that you can download, which outlines everything discussed herein. You'll find a link to it here so that you can follow along if you like as well as at the end of this book in Appendix A, but please do read the entire book first. Now, download your free, easy-to-reference safety checklist here.[1]

More Books You'll Enjoy

If you liked what you read when finished you can find more safety and survival books I've written at https://rethinksurvival.com/kindle-books/.[2]

This Book's Tone

As noted before, this book is written in a quick, simple, easy to read format. Hence, it is presented in a conversational form and not one that is intended to be grammatically correct. Keeping YOU and your loved ones safe is the sole focus of this book.

And My Thanks...

I also want to thank those folks who took the time to review this book, to offer their own suggestions, and to correct my mistakes. You know who you are.

Self-Defense Myths and Realities

Figure 1

Let's start this discussion with what most people think women's safety advice is all about: personal self-defense, so that we can get it out of the way and move on to actions that are far more likely to keep you safe.

Regrettably, if you're to the point where you must defend yourself from an attacker then odds are that something else went wrong—possibly even many things—and now you're down to this last-ditch effort to defend yourself. Now, before we get into what you can do in such a situation, you must first understand three crucial points about self-defense:

1. Women are almost always going to be physically outmatched by men.
2. Substance use makes fighting back more difficult from a female's perspective and a confrontation more likely from a male's perspective.
3. The movies get fight scenes all wrong.

Of course, I must concede that the first point—women are physically outmatched by men—is a generality regarding gender differences and that there are clearly exceptions to the rule. No doubt, there are women who are physically stronger than men as well as those who are more able to fight too. If you're truly one of the gifted few, you may choose to skip the first safety tip; all others should read on.

Regarding the Physicality of Men Versus Women

Believing that, on average, women are equally capable in a physical confrontation to men is a fallacy. I'm not trying to be sexist here whatsoever. On the contrary, I need you to understand and accept reality so that you don't make a poor choice down the road. In this case, believing that you, as a female, can stand toe-to-toe with most males in any sort of physical confrontation.

You see, men really are built differently and are more physically capable than women. For starters, in the United States men are, on average, five inches taller than women and twenty-five to thirty pounds heavier, according to these respective Wikipedia entries here and here.[3,4] That may not seem like much, but these differences manifest in vastly different ways, particularly muscle mass.

This article explains it best: "Studies have proven again and again that men have a greater amount of skeletal muscle than women. In one such study that examined 468 men and women... researchers determined that men had an average of 72.6 pounds of muscle compared to the 46.2 pounds found in women. The men had 40 percent more muscle mass in the upper body and 33 percent more in the lower body."[5] The article went on to state that even a man's muscles are five to ten percent stronger than a woman's muscles, pound for pound.

Moreover, there is something to be said for hormonal differences, particularly relative testosterone levels—the hormone causally related to muscle growth—in men versus women. This article points out that, "Healthy males who have gone through puberty have 20 times the levels of testosterone compared to a healthy female."[6] Such glaring differences cannot be ignored. Anecdotally, when a man's testosterone spikes or he's on an adrenaline rush then he's often capable of much greater physical feats than ordinary and feels little to no pain in the moment.

Put simply: most males are significantly larger and stronger than most females and are, therefore, more capable in a physical confrontation due, in part, to far greater testosterone levels which allow for greater feats of strength as well as higher levels of momentary pain tolerance.

Regarding Substance Use

Substance use, especially alcohol use, slows a person's reaction times, reduces hand-eye coordination, and generally makes for poor decision making at any given moment. And since we've already established that women are, on average, less capable than men in a physical confrontation, substance use will further degrade one's ability to fight back when needed the most.

In addition, violent crimes tend to be related to substance abuse by men.[7] An intoxicated man or, worse, one who is using hardcore drugs such as PCP or methamphetamines, tend to make them more aggressive and, as such, more likely to seek a physical confrontation than they otherwise might. Plus, because alcohol and drugs numb the senses men are even more impervious to pain when using them.

Don't believe me? Just search YouTube for videos like *man on drugs fights off cops* and you'll find plenty of instances where even multiple police officers have a difficult time bringing down a single man who is apparently high or intoxicated. If you, no matter what you believe you're currently capable of, believe that you can do a better job than multiple, trained police officers of subduing a man who feels almost no pain and has no fear then you're simply kidding yourself.

Regarding Movie Fight Scenes

Unfortunately, movies and television shows just aren't doing us any good when it comes to realistic fight scenes, particularly the ones where our heroine fights off half a dozen bad guys with ease. That's just not based in any sort of reality whatsoever. For instance, most people won't be incapacitated with a single punch or kick to the face as movie fight scenes often depict. While a lucky blow is possible, such as with a blow to one's temple, most of the time what we see on television is a complete fantasy. Again, watch a few YouTube videos of actual street fights and you'll see what I mean.

Therefore, please don't believe that a martial arts or self-defense class is going to teach you how to throw a punch to the face that will knock out your assailant cold. At the very least, such a class will teach you how and where to strike with surprise and with enough force so that you then have a chance to flee. At best, self-defense classes will also teach you how to be assertive and, most importantly, how to be situationally aware of your surroundings. Knowing these strategies are what will truly save your life.

Three Points of Emphasis Regarding Self-Defense

First, this article explains that: "Whether or not you have self-defense training, and no matter what your age or physical condition, it is important to understand that you CAN and SHOULD defend yourself physically. You have both the moral and legal right to do so, even if the attacker is only threatening you and hasn't struck first. Many women worry that they will anger the attacker and get hurt worse if they defend themselves, but statistics clearly show that your odds of survival are far greater if you do fight back."[8]

Second, this article points out that: "'Every predator has two fears: getting caught or getting hurt,' Kardian said. 'When you don't act as the predator expects you to, you ruin his plan.' One way to fight back is to be verbal. 'Let them know you know they're there,' he said. 'Calling them out might cause them to back off.' And even if a predator says, 'Don't scream or yell,' women should still be vocal,' Kardian said. 'Yelling or screaming will attract attention, which can save your life.'"[9]

Third, the article continues: "'Men who physically assault women will use their size, strength and terror tactics to subdue a woman,' Soalt said. 'The goal to fighting back is to escape.' Soalt said women should not struggle against an assailant's greatest strengths. 'You'll just exhaust yourself,' she said. Instead, wait for the moment when he's distracted. 'A man will close in on your space, so use that close proximity to strike back,' she said. Use simple, primal moves — strike the eyes, throat or groin — or use the heel of both of your palms to clap him hard on both ears, which will disorient him. 'Any move you make has to be 100 percent so you have a chance to run,' she said. 'Make sure it's explosive.'"[10]

I couldn't have said it better myself, but let me reiterate the following:

1. You do have the moral and legal right to defend yourself if threatened with harm.
2. Be verbal regardless of what the attacker says as doing so draws unwanted attention which plays into their fear of getting caught.
3. Your goal is always to escape. Wait for the right moment when he's distracted to strike and then run away.

So long as you fully appreciate the physical differences in genders and how these differences put women at a disadvantage, you'll be more likely to make a wise decision when faced with a physical confrontation.

Now, let move on to what's really going to keep you safe from harm.

Safety Tip # 1: Your Awareness is Crucial

I'm sure most experts will agree that being aware of your surroundings, who's near you, who may be eyeing you, what may be ahead of you, and so on are crucial to ensuring one's safety regardless of gender. Being aware of what's going on around you is easily more important than anything else you can do to ensure your personal safety day in and day out.

For instance, the simple act of noticing a man approaching you from your blind spot because you had your head on a swivel may be enough of a deterrent for the would-be attacker to change their mind or for you to take appropriate action.

In addition, the mere act of you being aware of your surroundings may cause you to change your plans, move to the other side of the street, or even to return to where you came from because, in your gut, you didn't feel safe.

Unfortunately, in today's modern society we're more distracted than ever by our electronics and all that they offer. **Do yourself a favor: put the phone away until you're in a truly safe place to look at it**. If you simply must look at your phone, take a moment to look around and see who or what may be headed your way because, after all, it isn't just predators who are a danger to you as distracted drivers, bicyclists, and plain bad luck strike at the worst moments too.

Safety Tip # 2: Take a Self-Defense Class

Knowing and practicing how to do something—anything—to defend yourself is better than knowing nothing at all. With that in mind, take a quality self-defense class. Although you won't become the next Bruce Lee, you will understand how, where, and when to strike an assailant. A good class will also discuss your situational awareness, allow you to practice being assertive with clear verbal skills and, of course, to practice being physical which is something many women shy away from.

Be sure the class includes realistic simulation scenarios—as much as can be attained without anyone getting hurt—and consider re-taking a class every year or two to ensure your skills stay fresh. Also, be aware that not all self-defense classes are created equal. Some classes are only an hour or two long, others last for weeks. Some are taught by male instructors, others by a female. Some are expensive, others are free. Do your research before making a choice because there are significant differences in how they teach.

If you need help, reach out to a local rape crisis center, police station, community college, or nearby YMCA as they sometimes offer classes to the public, often for a reasonable price. Once you've narrowed down options, talk to the instructor beforehand to get a better sense of what to expect.

Safety Tip # 3: Consider Self-Paced Instruction

If you cannot take a class due to time constraints then consider learning a few self-defense moves on your own. For instance, I once reviewed the B.E.T. Target Based Self-Defense System DVD by David Alexander and enjoyed his approach very much.[11] I even had my kids practice along with me at the time. If interested, it appears you can get the system for significantly less than what I recall when I reviewed it and you can even watch the course online via Udemy, if you like.[12]

Surely there are many other DVD-based or online self-defense courses available as well as plenty of free videos online if you prefer. I link to dozens of personal defense videos on my website here, many of which discuss Krav Maga techniques along with a variety of self-defense maneuvers for both men and women, and plenty more.[13] Or do a search on YouTube for *self-defense techniques for women* and you'll find many videos to choose from.

Clearly, there are drawbacks to practicing on your own, including not having someone to correct your mistakes, a greater likelihood of you or others getting hurt, and you'll be less likely to take the ideas and techniques seriously because you don't have a realistic scenario to go by. I only suggest you practice on your own if you have no other option. Finally, you're not trying to learn an entire new martial art system or complicated techniques. Keep it simple.

Safety Tip # 4: The Most Vulnerable Body Parts

The most vulnerable points on the body are the groin, eyes, and front of the throat. These are the very same areas that the B.E.T. system mentioned previously targets. Know that if you're going to strike these vulnerable points then do so with everything you've got because you'll likely only get one chance and, besides, you really are attempting to incapacitate your attacker, not just to momentarily hurt them.

Realize, though, that most men will instinctively react to protect their groin area so you probably shouldn't attempt to strike there first unless you have no better option. Go for the eyes or throat instead. And if you're going to strike the eyes or throat then you *need* to do so with more force than you realize, because you really are trying to literally push their eyes into the back of their head or to punch through to their spine from the front of the neck. I know it sounds gruesome, but this is the only way that I am aware of to force an attacker to involuntarily stop what they're doing. You *need* to be exceedingly forceful.

The important part to remember is that you don't want to be trading punches with an attacker, especially a man. Strike their most vulnerable parts of the body once or twice if the opportunity arises and then get out of there.

Safety Tip # 5: If Grabbed Unexpectedly

For starters, if you're ever assaulted in such a way then you should immediately begin shouting *stop* at the top of your lungs as if your life depends on it because it very well could. Some suggest yelling *fire* instead as that word is more likely to attract attention than either stop or help will be. The important part is being extremely vocal to attract attention. What to do after that will depend on how you're grabbed:

If *grabbed from behind as in a bearhug* try to bite their hands, kick their shins in a downward motion, then drop straight to the ground. You want to be as difficult as humanly possible to hold onto, so much so that they'll prefer to let go.

If *grabbed from behind with a neck chokehold*, you first need to grab the arm you're being choked with for better control of your movements and then, if possible, step to the side and strike the man's groin with a hand or foot; this video shows what to do.[14] If that's not possible, I would suggest a quick upward strike to the nose because that's probably the only other relatively vulnerably place you'll have a chance to strike in this position.

If *grabbed from the front by your arm or wrist*, lift and twist your arm away from the palm because where a man's fingers come together is always the weakest point of contact. Sometimes it helps to use your other hand to grab the one that's being held for additional force when attempting to break a grip.

If *your hair is grabbed from the front* the technique gets a bit more difficult to explain, but the idea is to first control the hand grabbing your hair by placing one hand atop the assailant's hand on your head, punch the inner elbow of the arm grabbing you, and then follow-up with a quick elbow or foot strike to the groin; this video explains the motions better.[15]

If *your hair is grabbed from the back* then consider it to be like the aforementioned neck chokehold, although any strikes will be more difficult to perform unless you purposefully take a step backwards toward your assailant which will be counterintuitive in a fight or flight situation.

Honestly, if you're unlucky enough to be grabbed in any manner by a relatively large man then odds are that you won't be able to do much of anything because they'll be able to severely restrict your movements due to overwhelming size and strength. In this case, scream, bite, kick, headbutt, and squirm as much as possible until they hopefully decide you're too much trouble. If you still have no luck, stop struggling for a moment and wait for a better opportunity to try again. In either case, yell and scream at the top of your lungs no matter what because attracting attention is a primary deterrent.

Safety Tip # 6: Personal Defense Tools

I'm sure you've heard of pepper spray, a stun gun, and a Taser before. These are the traditional options for most women, although there are others such as the tactical pen which works as a real pen and is TSA-compliant, kubotan, neck knives, and more. They're often touted as *the solution* to keeping you safe from danger, whether that's walking to your car after a shopping trip or jogging around the neighborhood.

Regrettably, nearly every personal defense tool has drawbacks. For instance, a stun gun or tactical pen requires you to be within arm's length to use, a Taser's barbs may not penetrate thick clothing, and traditional pepper spray can blow back in your face thereby inadvertently incapacitating you. Besides, any tool is useless to you unless it's physically in your hand during an attack and you're ready, willing, and capable of using one to defend yourself. Most people will simply stop carrying their defensive tool of choice after a few days simply because it's inconvenient.

Even so, I would still encourage you to purchase something to keep readily accessible somewhere because there may be times when you feel the need to have a self-defense tool with you which is impossible if you have nothing to begin with. Furthermore, if you keep a defensive tool in your purse or vehicle then it should always be available most times when you leave the house.

You could, of course, simply keep your weapon of choice in a purse assuming you carry one, but these types of items tend to get buried in the bottom relatively quickly. Keeping something readily available on your keychain or in your car ensures it's always in the same place and more readily accessible in most situations when you're away from home.

Which tool to get?

If I had to choose between these three main options, pepper spray gel is usually the best one because it (1) works on most people, (2) typically has a longer range than traditional pepper spray or foam, and (3) is legal in all fifty states, although there are restrictions on possession, use, and more.[16] Please research state and local laws just to be sure.[17]

Where to keep the cannister?

Your keychain might be a good option if the cannister is small enough. If you prefer the car then I would avoid keeping it in the glove box, center console, or anywhere that must be opened to access. Secured somewhere on the driver's door, like the door pull handle, may be a good choice as this allows for ready access. If you have young children then consider a safer location, most likely on your person. Finally, pepper spray storage temperatures need to be below 120 degrees Fahrenheit and out of the sun to avoid leakage concerns.[18]

21

Safety Tip # 7: Safety Whistles and Alarms

What about carrying a whistle or loud personal alarm? Although both my wife and I carry a whistle, we only do so for disaster preparedness purposes, for example, being stuck in an elevator or becoming trapped inside of a building. Using a whistle saves your voice when needing to signal for help, is much louder, and carries further too. Plus, a simple keychain whistle is virtually unnoticeable and always with you when you leave the house.[19] I highly recommend you carry one for this purpose.

For personal safety I doubt a whistle will do you much good unless you (1) have it readily accessible in your hand at all times and (2) there are plenty of other people around to hear it, in which case yelling or screaming will likely suffice. The same advice can be said for those 130db+ personal alarms that are intended to be attached to your keychain. I don't recommend either option.

If you're going to focus on carrying something in your hand for safety then I would suggest you have something that can actually be useful for your personal defense such as the aforementioned pepper spray gel or whichever tool you prefer. Later, I discuss carrying a specific flashlight for self-defense purposes which could be a useful alternative with the added benefit of providing you with a handy source of light for nighttime outings.

Safety Tip # 8: The Fight or Flight Response

I'm sure you've heard of the fight or flight response before. It's what causes you to freeze from fright and makes your heart figuratively jump out of your chest when you're scared. It's also what gives you the ability to fight back by dumping adrenaline into your system when you feel threatened. These reactions are triggered by your Amygdala, a tiny almond-shaped, ancient portion of your brain.

Details aside, the Amygdala reacts faster than your prefrontal cortex which means that a person's fight or flight response is involuntary and immediate. You simply don't have a choice in how you initially react in a moment of terror. This is both good and bad because it means that in moments of real danger, like needing to jump out of the way of a moving vehicle, you'll react immediately, but it could also be bad if you have a tendency to freeze in frightening situations. My guess is you know which one you are.

If you're the take action sort of person, you'll be in better shape to deal with such problems. If, on the other hand, you're not that way then a moment's hesitation could be awfully bad for you. The only way I know to combat or retrain your Amygdala's preprogrammed response is with practice. With regards to your personal safety, that means practicing self-defense techniques in specific scenarios, like being grabbed from behind, and doing so regularly.

Additional Self-Defense Considerations

Safety Tip # 9: Carry Car Keys in Your Hand

Some people suggest carrying car keys in your hand in such a way as to use them for self-defense with a few keys poking out between clenched fingers. Personally, I wouldn't suggest doing so because this technique is probably not as easy as it looks and no more effective than using any other self-defense tool like pepper spray. The real reason to carry keys in your hand is so that you're not wasting time fumbling through your purse or bag for them.

Safety Tip # 10: Make Eye Contact, Speak Up

Don't be afraid to make eye contact or to speak up, even loudly, if someone is getting too close or making you feel uncomfortable. Doing so ensures they know you're not an easy target and speaking up draws unwanted attention from bystanders. Plus, criminals understand that they're more easily identified if they know you've had a good look at them. That said, you don't want to come off as being overly aggressive or, heaven-forbid, flirty either. I'd imagine it's a fine line to walk as a woman so use your best judgment.

Safety Tip # 11: Use Your Elbow

Your elbow is the strongest point on the body. If you're unable to strike the most vulnerable parts of the body—the eyes, throat, and groin—then strike the bridge of the nose, sides of the head at the temples, back or sides of the neck, or sides of the knee as the best alternative locations to target.

Safety Tip # 12: If You Have Long Hair

Long hair—particularly hair pulled back into a ponytail—is easier to grab and control. Consider putting your hair up when going out instead. If that's too much trouble you could still bunch a ponytail together with a scrunchie so that there's less to grab.

Safety Tip # 13: If Facing Multiple Aggressors

While the typical assumption is that there will only be one assailant, what happens if there are two or more? Nothing good, that's for sure. If you find yourself being targeted in some manner by multiple men then you must remove yourself from the situation as quickly as possible since groups of men tend to act even more emboldened than they would alone.

Of course, this depends on the situation. While it's one thing to brush off and move away from a group of intoxicated men who are probably being inappropriate towards you, it's quite another to brush off a group of men who may have worse intentions like robbing you. You'll have to decide how best to proceed.

Realize, too, that fighting off a group of men is almost impossible. You need to use your wits. Be as polite, yet as direct, as you can be while moving away. If necessary, be assertive with your voice and actions, telling them to stay away from your personal space while simultaneously attempting to get the attention of any bystanders.

Safety Tip # 14: If They're Wielding a Firearm

Experts suggest that it is very unlikely you will be hit if an assailant even does attempt to shoot, and that the odds of them hitting a vital organ are even less.[20] The fact is that displaying a firearm is usually only an empty threat designed to get you to comply. That's not always the case, of course, such as if a weapon is later pulled because you're not initially complying or if you've been aggressive towards the assailant in your defense.

Typically, the best plan is to run away as fast as possible before the shooter has time to react. Know that running in a zig-zag patten as is often touted as the best course of action isn't any more effective at avoiding being hit than simply running away as fast as possible.[21] There may be some minor advantages to running zig-zig, but not many. Just run.

Safety Tip # 15: Should You Carry a Firearm?

I know people who choose to carry a concealed firearm anytime they leave the house—sometimes even around the house—and not all of them are men. This, clearly, is a personal choice and one not to be taken lightly. If you are interested in doing so, realize that there are many firearm options available and plenty of good people willing to help you find the right one for you. Just visit a local gun shop and you'll be amazed at all they have to offer.

Furthermore, if you do choose to carry a firearm for self-defense then you really do need to get appropriate training so that you can (1) use the firearm effectively for its intended purpose and (2) not be a danger to yourself or others. And, of course, you must follow the law, including obtaining an appropriate concealed carry permit and abiding by gun-free laws at schools and government buildings, to name two obvious gun-free locations.

Safety Tip # 16: Carry a Flashlight Instead

If a firearm isn't quite your style and even pepper spray gel feels like a bit much, how about a flashlight intended for self-defense? An example would be this handheld WOWTAC BSS 4 Tactical Flashlight.[22] Not only is it a bright flashlight which is always smart to have on your person, but it's also useful for self-defense purposes because it includes a screw-on strike bezel. Plus, the flashlight is rechargeable, can run for many hours, and is highly water-resistant. The only major drawback is that you must be within arm's length to use it for self-defense purposes. Watch this video discussing the features if you'd like more information.[23]

Self-Defense Takeaways

Ultimately, all self-defense techniques and tools require some level of competent, regular practice. Take the time now and learn how to use the tools and techniques properly, safely, and legally. Here's what else you need to remember:

- Men are typically stronger and more capable in a fight than women. Don't attempt to stand toe-to-toe unless you have no other choice.

- Assailants are often fueled by substance use which makes them even more illogical and difficult to fight off.

- You have the moral and legal right to defend yourself when clearly threatened.

- Predators fear getting caught and being hurt. Yell and scream to draw attention and fight back with everything you've got if you must.

- Remember that the goal of fighting back is to allow you to escape. Strike fast and strong, then run. This isn't the movies.

- Awareness of your surroundings is crucial. Trust your gut and don't be afraid to avoid a situation for fear of insulting others.

- Take a quality self-defense class or, at the very least, learn some easier moves on your own.

- Practice makes perfect. Ensure you practice your self-defense moves regularly so they stay fresh in your mind and, of course, always keep everyone's safety in mind when you do practice because it's easy to get hurt if you're not careful or practicing unsupervised.

- The elbow is the strongest point on your body. Use it to strike vulnerable points on your assailant such as the bridge of the nose, temples, back or sides of the neck, and sides of the knees.
- Get a self-defense tool of your choice and keep it in on your person, keychain, or even in your car. I suggest pepper spray gel for a few key reasons, but anything is better than nothing. Even a tactical flashlight or pen could be useful for this purpose if you prefer something more practical.
- Making eye contact lets an assailant know you're paying attention and potentially gives them pause for fear of later being identified.
- If facing an assailant with a firearm, just run. Fast. Most times they're only shown to get you to comply, so if they want your purse then toss it one way and you run the other.

Remember that self-defense isn't about winning a fight. Rather, it's solely about giving you the opportunity to escape or, at the very least, for the assailant to decide you're too much trouble. Choose to make yourself as much trouble as possible. Better yet, reduce the likelihood of such encounters by making smart decisions with whom and where you frequent.

Safety at Home

Figure 2

Feeling safe in your own home is a right that everyone should enjoy, and even more so in our modern society. Sadly, we're not actually as safe as we think we are. For example, windows can be easily broken with a rock, doors may be readily kicked in with a strike of one's foot or forced open using a crowbar, and home invasions are on the rise. What's a safety-conscious woman (or man) to do?

Fortunately, there are plenty of useful actions on can take. For now, we'll focus on the major ones that are intended to keep you safe from bodily harm whether you're home alone or not.

Safety Tip # 17: Lock Doors and Windows

I know people who still don't lock their front door at times. In fact, according to this article, "63% of surveyed Americans said they know people who don't lock their house doors regularly," and that, "30% of all burglaries occur with the offender entering through an unlocked door."[24]

Of course, we're not interested in stopping burglars here, but if a person can get into your home as easily as walking right in the front door or crawling through an unlocked window, you're just asking for trouble. After all, who's to say what this person really wants? Perhaps all they wanted initially was to steal your jewelry, but then the situation quickly devolved because you were unexpectedly home and now they felt the need to attack you to escape.

To make matter worse, oftentimes these people are on drugs or looking to score more which means they're not thinking clearly to start with. And if you wrongly believe that you can reason your way out of things, trust me when I say that rational thinking will not be a burglar's strongest attribute in the moment.

There's no reason to make it any easier on the bad guys, so lock your doors and windows. All of them should be locked as often as possible—even when home—unless you're airing out the room you're in for an hour or two.

Safety Tip # 18: Make It Clear Someone Appears to be Home

While you may want it to look like nobody's home when it comes to you avoiding bodily harm, that's not the case. Most burglars don't want a confrontation whatsoever which means you should make it clear that somebody is home, especially when you really are. In so doing, they'll be far more likely to move along and never even bother to investigate your home or who's inside any further. Granted, there are exceptions, such as those intent on committing a home invasion, but most of the time making it look obvious that somebody is home is the best way to stay safe. With that in mind, here's a few thoughts:

1. Keep lights and a television or radio on, even during the day, since criminals will assume that somebody must be home if there's a lot of noise and activity going on inside.
2. Park a vehicle in the driveway and be sure to keep the doors locked and windows rolled shut as well as any valuables, including the garage door opener, out of sight.
3. Get a dog as they tend to make noise which attracts unwanted attention. Remember that criminals don't want anyone to notice them, neither homeowners nor neighbors. Besides, dogs make for welcome company.

Safety Tip # 19: Make it Obvious Criminals Might Get Caught Later

According to various criminal's statements, "About 60% of the burglars indicated that the presence of an alarm would cause them to seek an alternative target altogether. This was particularly true among the subset of burglars that were more likely to spend time deliberately and carefully planning a burglary."[25]

In addition, there were more than a few articles which stated that, "the most effective deterrents for home burglaries and car theft were CCTV [closed circuit television] cameras…" according to those burglars interviewed.[26] Regardless, working cameras are always touted as one of the two best ways to deter crime no matter who you ask or where you live. Thus, adding obvious to see and functional cameras is an easy deterrent to make use of, even if it's as simple as a Ring doorbell camera.

It should be clear by now that most criminals don't want to be caught, even days later, let alone possibly caught in the act by police. Therefore, installing a functioning alarm system and security cameras are, without a doubt, two of the most useful deterrents available to us. Moreover, it stands to reason that if alarm systems and cameras are useful to thwart burglaries, then they should also be useful to deter home invasions, so long as they're clearly functional.

Safety Tip # 20: Avoiding Home Invasions

Unfortunately, statistics vary widely as many authorities still don't report home invasions separate from home burglaries. As such, it's hard to pinpoint just how many home invasions occur each year. That said, they do seem to be on the rise. Why? This article suggests that they're on the rise for two main reasons: "The first is that regular home burglary is rapidly becoming more difficult because of home security cameras and social media. Historically only 13% of all home burglaries are solved. But that is rapidly changing with homeowners using surveillance cameras to take pictures of the perpetrators and posting them on social media."[27] Clearly, our own efforts to put a stop to home burglaries are forcing criminals to get more desperate and bolder.

The article goes on to suggest that the other big reason home invasions are on the rise is for a criminal to fuel their drug habit which is, from what I've seen, a big reason for home burglaries to begin with. Worse, because many of the people who commit home invasions are hooked on drugs or intoxicated, they're clearly not thinking logically and may even be hallucinating or highly irrational. None of that is good news for you if you expect to talk your way out of a horrible ordeal, as stated previously.

So, what can you do? The major takeaways to know are this:

34

1. Upgrade your front door security, specifically with a long-throw deadbolt and hardened door strike plate, if possible. You should then use three-inch screws to secure the door hinges.

2. Add secondary locks, such as a security bar, to avoid your door either being kicked in if you chose not to open the door or forced opened when you do answer. Do this for every exterior door, but the front door is your primary concern.

3. Install a wide-angle peephole so you can more clearly see if anyone is hiding off to the side and consider installing a home security camera at the front door so you can see and record who's there.

4. Respond to the door, but don't open it. You may be tempted not to say anything or pretend you're not home, but criminals are getting more brazen and may be willing to enter if you don't answer because they assume nobody is home. Be assertive and say, "Who is it?" Let them know you won't be answering the door and then call the authorities if you're truly suspicious.

5. Be vigilant for whom and why you open the door and never trust clean-cut, good looking men. Age isn't a factor either. In fact, you're better off never opening the door unless you're sure who is on the other side no matter what they say or how desperate they seem to be. Sadly, some criminals have been known to impersonate city workers or even use crying females to get people to open their doors. Don't fall for it.

What if They Attempt Entry?

If criminals do gain entry or are attempting to do so then a good plan is to run, hide, and fight, as this video recommends.[28] While calling 9-1-1 attempt to escape through a backdoor or window. If that's not possible then hide somewhere like a barricaded bedroom or even a bathroom with a solid, sturdy door because typical interior doors are easily kicked through. This means that you'll need to replace the entire door. You should then install a deadbolt and use longer, three-inch screws to contact the studs as mentioned previously. In addition, employ a secondary door brace, such as security bar or door jammer, to further resist entry. Pretend like this door is your front door and you'll get the idea.

Additionally, this room is your safe room where you wait for the police to respond. It would also be a good idea to include a separate prepaid and activated cell phone in this room in case you don't have yours as you retreat, though, a landline would be the best choice if you still pay for the service. It couldn't hurt to open the window and scream for help. Last, if forced to do so, fight the intruders with anything and everything you have, including the use of deadly force. Whether you choose to have a firearm in this room for self-defense is up to you, but you should have some defensive option available. Even a large cannister of pepper spray gel is better than nothing.

Additional Safety Considerations at Home

Safety Tip # 21: Don't Display Your Name Publicly

Never put your name on any signage where you live such as the mailbox or apartment buzzer. Doing so makes it potentially easier for a would-be criminal to look up your personal information online—even your social security number—with a previously stolen credit card right there on the spot. Criminals may be able to discover your place of employment and even discern whether you're married or not. Knowing such information may embolden them to act when they otherwise might not have.

Safety Tip # 22: Make Noise When You're Home

Any sort of noise, even that of a television or radio, is often a deterrent to criminals as it indicates people are home. Remember that most criminals don't want a confrontation whatsoever which means you're better off indicating you are home.

Safety Tip # 23: Moving Bags Into Your Home

When moving bags or packages into your home be sure to lock the house door upon entering each time. I know that can be a pain to remember to do, but it's better to be safe than sorry.

On a similar note, you should consider taking the garage door opener with you if you have one since they're easy to snatch out of an open vehicle. You might wrongly assume that you misplaced the opener only to find out that a burglar returned later that night. After all, most people don't assume these things are so easily stolen which makes garage door openers a better target for thieves than even keys.

Safety Tip # 24: Keep Trees and Bushes Trimmed

Keep bushes and trees trimmed to reduce potential hiding spots, particularly near doors, windows, and fences because criminals aren't only hiding from you, but from your neighbors too.

Safety Tip # 25: Install Motion Sensing Lights

Leaving the porch light on at night is typically a bad idea because it signals to thieves that nobody is home. But having no outside lighting is unsafe for anyone. Instead, consider adding motion-activated floodlights around your home, particularly where you're most likely to be entering including the driveway, front porch, and garage. And remember to cover areas where a criminal might be hiding, such as the side of the house or detached garage.

Safety Tip # 26: Keep Your Distance With Deliveries

Deliveries, including food, should be left for you to pick up later at your own convenience. Perhaps the only exception would be those deliveries that require a signature or immediate payment, and even then you should *only* open the door and accept it if you are expecting the delivery. If you're unsure and the delivery person is insistent, err on the side of caution and don't open the door. Deliveries can almost always return later no matter what they say.

Safety Tip # 27: If You Lose Your House Keys

Consider changing your exterior door locks if your house keys are lost and certainly if they're stolen. Remember to do so quickly because criminals know that time is of the essence. In the meantime, I would suggest you utilize secondary door locks or braces as mentioned in the home invasion safety tip until you can get the situation remedied.

Also, instead of replacing the deadbolts which can get quite expensive, oftentimes your local hardware store can rekey existing cylinders for much less cost if you bring them in; they're not hard to remove. Of course, you may have to purchase a single, new deadbolt so they have a different key to utilize, but that sure beats replacing multiple door lock cylinders which would all have to be rekeyed anyway.

Safety Tip # 28: When Moving Into a New Rental

Do two things when moving into a new rental: (1) check smoke alarms and any leftover decorations for hidden cameras when you first move in and (2) ask that all exterior door locks be changed because even if all house keys were turned in by a previous tenant, they can be easily duplicated.

Safety at Home Takeaways

Your safety at home is mostly about routines such as taking the garage door opener with you when you get home, but also about reducing the likelihood of you being targeted for some easy to fix reason like not posting signage with your name on it. Here's what else you need to remember:

- You're almost always better off indicating that someone is home by making noise, but don't make it any easier on criminals by leaving doors or windows unlocked either.
- Ensure criminals don't have any easy places to hide, so keep your trees and bushes well-trimmed and install motion sensing lights where it makes sense.
- Getting caught is a major concern for most criminals. As such, you should consider installing a real alarm system—remember to use it religiously—along with security cameras. Neither of these can be fake or merely window decals; criminals can spot the difference and if you ever did need them you'll be kicking yourself for not getting the real deal.
- Be vigilant with your actions, from locking the door behind you when taking bags inside to keeping your distance when accepting deliveries, it all makes a difference in reducing bad outcomes.

Safety Around the Neighborhood

Figure 3

Aside from your home and vehicle, most people expect to feel safe around the neighborhood, so much so that we tend to let our guard down anywhere near our home. After all, you likely know the neighbors, they know you, things are usually quiet, and everyone seems friendly.

There are times when this isn't the case. I'm sure you've had a situation in your past that didn't feel quite right or made you uneasy. Various women in my life have had odd encounters and, thankfully, nothing ever resulted from them. Were they being overly paranoid? I couldn't say, but I am glad that they were vigilant and a bit standoffish in the moment. Luck aside, vigilance is key. So are your routines. Let's discover how together.

Safety Tip # 29: Stay Off Your Phone When Out

I know this will be difficult for many people—especially for the younger generation—but if there is *one distraction* above all others that will take away your attention from what's going on around you, it's your smartphone and all that it offers.

The problem is that everyone I know, probably even me at times, will often be on their phone while out walking the neighborhood. Both my wife and mother are guilty of talking on their phones or scrolling through Facebook while walking the dog. My son is always texting or playing music with earbuds stuck in his ears, sometimes doing both. And I often see other folks doing the exact same things.

The biggest problem with these distractions isn't about avoiding being assaulted, as one might suspect. Rather, it's more about your lack of awareness of vehicles around you because, let's be honest, some people drive like idiots through neighborhood streets. They drive too fast, may be distracted by their own smartphone use, and expect *you* to be paying attention to *them*.

And if you're not looking up because your eyes are glued to the phone or you can't hear what may be coming around the corner because you've got earbuds in then you're putting your safety at greater risk because you're relying solely on drivers to be doing the right thing themselves or to react in time.

Sadly, each year thousands of pedestrians are killed and tens of thousands injured and the numbers appear to be rising, according to a recent study which states: "'We are crazy distracted,' says Melody Geraci, deputy executive director of the Active Transportation Alliance, a Chicago group advocating for better walking, cycling and public transportation options. 'After speeding and the failure to yield, distractions are the number three cause [of pedestrian fatalities], particularly by electronic devices.'" The article goes on to point out that: "Drivers distracted by their devices are a well-documented, rising cause of traffic crashes, but there are a growing number of pedestrians, too, who can become oblivious to traffic around them."[29]

Clearly, anyone who wishes to assault you will rely on you being distracted by your phone as well. No doubt, being on your phone is a major distraction anywhere, not just while you're out walking or jogging. As an example, being on your phone even while parked in the car can be just as dangerous as we'll discover soon enough. The same can be said for anywhere that you may be vulnerable such as stairwells, the elevator, and parking garages, to name a few places where you should stay off the phone whenever possible, particularly when you're alone.

Safety Tip # 30: Walk With Someone Else

A seemingly easy solution to staying off your phone would be to walk with somebody else. This could be anyone, from a friend or neighbor, to your spouse or a child. Doing so will surely make you safer, partly because there is safety in numbers, and will likely keep you off your smartphone and engaged in conversation which, naturally, will keep your head up and ears perked. Plus, you may be more motivated to get out and walk or jog, thereby improving your fitness level if you know somebody else is relying on you to do so. It's a win-win.

Granted, if everyone who is out walking with you also has their heads buried in a phone then this idea won't help much. Now, I wouldn't go so far as to leave your phone at home in case you need to call someone for help or vice versa. Just keep the phone in your pocket most of the time where it belongs.

Why Your Dog Won't Defend You

Occasionally, I hear people say that their dog will protect them if they're at home or even out walking and are assaulted. I beg to differ.

Most dogs won't do anything useful to defend you against an attack. Even big, scary dogs aren't likely to do more than bark a lot. As an example, one news station decided to test whether a homeowner's dogs would do anything to stop a burglar from invading their home, stealing valuables, and even being near the family's children. Sadly, two of the three sets of test dogs, which included German Shepherds and a Rottweiler, did nothing as this article relates.[30] One dog did nip at the intruder when he came close to the homeowner, but they certainly didn't attack with fangs bared as the homeowners expected them to.

Why didn't the dogs do anything? After all, dogs are loyal and pack-oriented, aren't they?

The aforementioned news article sums it up nicely: "'To them [the dog], you're the caretaker, so if you're there, you should be the one taking care of them, not them taking care of you—like a child in your family,' Deputy Tucker said."

Of course, not every dog will react this way. Some dogs surely will defend their owners or home, and I'm willing to bet that you already know this because he or she has shown aggressive tendencies in the past. But if you've never seen that sort of behavior and merely hope that your dog will do something, don't bet your life on it because they probably won't lift a paw to defend you, your home, or your children. Their favorite chew toy may be a different story.

Perhaps the mere presence of a dog may be just enough of a deterrent for an assailant to reconsider but don't bet on it.

Safety Tip # 31: Switch Up Routines Regularly

This is something that my wife needs to do better, and perhaps you do as well if you walk or jog the neighborhood. For instance, my wife takes our dog on a walk in the morning when she gets up and usually again in the early evening, and she typically walks the same direction at around the same times. This, unfortunately, isn't being as vigilant as she can be.

What can she do better? For starters she could change the direction that she walks because she usually follows a loop in the neighborhood or, better yet, she could choose to walk completely different streets even though it throws off her preferred routine. In addition, she could vary the times significantly which does occasionally happen because she doesn't always walk the dog at the same time.

If you cannot vary your routine due to your work schedule or whatever, then just do your best to be extra vigilant including ensuring car doors are locked, staying off the phone, and keeping your head up.

Obviously, being unpredictable if someone is paying attention to your daily routines makes you less of a target. The more you can vary your routines the better, including times, routes, participants, and even entire activities. Besides, you'll be happier as well if you're not doing the same old thing day after day.

Safety Tip # 32: Use Smartphone Safety Apps

Most smartphone safety apps seem silly and useless, possibly even detrimental. I know I've tried various safety apps which seemed useful but were annoying as time went on. But a few apps do stand out and I'm sure more will have been developed by the time you read this. Please peruse the appropriate app store for something potentially better.

Although apps that can send automated safety messages to specific phone contacts sounds useful, I doubt they are. I remember one disaster safety app I tried allowed me to send an SOS by pressing the power key three times in quick succession. After having accidentally sent an errant SOS a few times over the course of two days, that app got deleted.

Even apps that allow for a single button push to dial 9-1-1 may not be of much use since most smartphones these days have an *emergency call* option accessible from the lock screen. Besides, if you're truly feeling unsafe in a situation then you should be calling 9-1-1 instead of fooling with some smartphone app.

Of course, there may be times when you want to be more discrete about reaching out for help. Thus, an app like Noonlight might be a viable choice because it can both silently summon help to your location, save details to your timeline, and more.[31]

If you merely want a location tracker app, Life360 is a good, free option and one that we've used for years.[32] There's no need to pay for the premium service; we've tried it for a year, and I found no obvious benefit beyond allowing for more alert notifications.

Another interesting option is the Watch Over Me app which allows you to simply shake your phone to begin video and audio recording and to alert contacts.[33] Plus, it can be set to begin recording at a specific time if you're having a meeting with someone you don't know as well as to share specific notes or a picture of someone such as being on a date, and more.

Ultimately, smartphone safety apps are only one of many tools in your personal safety arsenal. As such, they should never be relied upon to ease up on your situational awareness or other safety considerations which are, without a doubt, far more crucial than any technology could ever be.

Last, if you are going to employ any of the recommended apps, take the time to get to know how they work as well as what they can do for you. After all, you sure wouldn't want to realize that you don't know how an app works or that it won't don't what you expect when you need it most.

Additional Safety Considerations for Around the Neighborhood

Safety Tip # 33: Ensure the Phone Battery is Charged

Your phone will do you no good if it has a dead battery. You can't make calls or text and safety apps surely won't work either. Ensure your phone is charged whenever you leave the house. You may even want to take a portable USB charger with you as a backup charging option.

Personally, I treat my phone like my vehicle's gas tank, in that, when it reaches 50% then I charge it no matter what I'm doing, and I encourage my family to do the same. Sadly, they don't always heed my advice and one day they may pay for it or perhaps be more inconvenienced than necessary when it's so easy to keep their phone properly charged.

Safety Tip # 34: Avoid Wearing Earbuds When Walking

If you use earbuds while walking or running, consider using only one earbud so you can pay more attention to your surroundings. Better yet, consider a pair of open ear headphones so you can still hear what's around you. Doing so isn't just about keeping you safe from an attacker, but even more so that you may be able to hear approaching vehicles, bicyclists, other runners, and so on. Or leave the earbuds at home and listen to the sounds of the city or nature.

Safety Tip # 35: If You're Approached or Followed

Make it a habit of crossing to the other side of the road if it's safe to do so whenever anyone approaches and even if you're passing others while walking, for example. This way you'll have several feet of distance or more between you should you need to react.

If someone is following closely behind you, stop and pretend to make a phone call or use one of the safety apps. Then do whatever works for you to allow time for them to pass by. This way you'll be able to keep your eye on them.

Change directions abruptly if it appears that someone may be following you. It's relatively normal for people to change directions on foot in a neighborhood and, at minimum, shows others that you're unpredictable, maybe even paying attention to them.

Safety Tip # 36: Minimizing Discovery of Your Home

If you're concerned about someone finding out where you live, continue walking past your home or stop well short of it, then preoccupy yourself until the person has clearly moved on.

If the other person has stopped as well, don't feel obligated to go straight home. There's no harm in waiting but realize that the longer you wait the longer it looks like you might live nearby which is exactly what you're trying to avoid. Instead, consider continuing as if you had just stopped to check your phone messages or whatever, then double-back when it is obvious things are safe again.

Safety Tip # 37: Let Family or Friends Know You're Out

Ensure someone knows that you're going out for a run or to walk the dog, for example, as well as when you're expected to return. If you're going to be longer than anticipated then be sure to let them know so they're not wrongly concerned about your safety.

Safety Tip # 38: Avoid Potential Ambush Locations

If you live in a neighborhood without sidewalks, consider walking in the middle of the street if it's not a busy roadway. Doing so will help keep you safe from surprise attacks from the bushes or, as in our case, the tree line and allows you to move left or right more easily to avoid other problems. Of course, you'll need to pay even more attention to what's going on behind you, such as with approaching vehicles, because you wouldn't want to be run over trying to stay safe. If you don't feel safe walking in the middle of the street, even a few feet further away from the side of the road is undoubtedly better than not.

Last, if you must walk near potential hiding spots like a dense set of bushes, be extra vigilant as you pass by or, if possible, give the area a wide berth for a brief moment until you've passed by.

Safety Around the Neighborhood Takeaways

Safety around the neighborhood is mostly about your situational awareness. Trust your gut and act decisively and you'll be able to avoid almost any bad situation. Here's what else you need to remember:

- Your smartphone is more distracting than anything else. Put it in your pocket. I know, easier said than done. Remember, too, that you should ensure the battery is charged as the phone will do you no good if it's dead.
- Similarly, wearing earbuds can be almost as distracting as the smartphone itself. If you must, use only one earbud.
- Even if you're not concerned, it's a good idea to switch up your routines to keep things fresh and others guessing. Change the times you get out, the direction you go, who you walk with, where. You get the idea. Plus, it never hurts to let someone you trust know that you're out and when you're expected to return so they're not unnecessarily concerned about you.
- The most important advice when out around the house is to keep your head up, ears open, and eyes scanning for whatever could be heading your way. Fortunately, this will rarely be the creepy guy down the street; it's more likely to be the distracted teenager driver on *their* phone.

Safety While Driving and Around Vehicles

Figure 4

A 2016 AAA report finds that: "American drivers spend an average of more than 17,600 minutes behind the wheel each year, according to a new survey from the AAA Foundation for Traffic Safety."[34]

Fortunately, it's not the amount of time we spend driving that affects our personal safety, it's the instances where we make ourselves vulnerable without realizing it that make the difference. You see, people feel safe in their vehicles. It's our home away from home if you will. We spend time with family and friends in the car, chauffer our kids everywhere they need to be, talk on the phone, eat, and more.

All of us, men included, tend to let our guard down once we close the car door behind us. We're often in a hurry to get somewhere else, maybe it's bitterly cold outside and we take a few minutes to warm up, or we just want to take a moment to respond to a text message. Whatever the reason, most of us mistakenly believe we're untouchable once inside the perceived safety of a vehicle.

Regrettably, unsuspecting men and women are assaulted every day in their vehicles. Carjacking, as with home invasions, is another crime on the rise. For instance, this article points out that: "The areas where these attempts were made are more often than not in parking lots of businesses and apartments, at intersections when the person stops for a traffic signal and at schools."[35]

Clearly, these attacks come when you're least likely to be paying attention, even while waiting to pick up children from school. In fact, most anytime you're interacting with your vehicle in some manner likely means you're distracted, from hurrying to your car to get to work on time or trying to get uncooperative children into the backseat, the possibility of begin assaulted at that moment is usually not on your mind.

Unfortunately, criminals know this and will take advantage of our being distracted. You need to turn the tables and avoid becoming their next target.

Safety Tip # 39: Lock Car Doors Immediately

Whenever you get into a vehicle, lock the doors. You may even go so far as to lock the doors when you're transitioning from one side of the vehicle to the other, such as when buckling a child into a car seat, for example. Once everyone is inside, always lock the doors no matter whether you're leaving your home or workplace, returning from a shopping trip or grocery store run, and certainly in poorly lit parking lots.

It's shocking how quickly criminals strike, often within seconds. Believe it or not, they're smarter than most of us law-abiding citizens give them credit for. They're waiting for that one person who is clearly distracted by their phone or children and then they make their move, often approaching from a blind spot so you never see them coming.

Think it can't happen to you? One carjacking victim recounted: "It happened so fast. Somebody hit on my trunk and the guy had the back door open. I turned around and just said, 'What's going on?'"[36] That's how fast these encounters happen.

Parking lots, in particular, make us exceptionally vulnerable because we expect to see people walking around and, therefore, aren't as suspicious of others near us and our car. That said, don't underestimate a determined criminal to brazenly walk right up to you and demand your car or purse when stopped at an intersection or stop sign, filling up at a gas station, returning from a restaurant outing or, worse, while you're waiting to get your child from school. If this ever does happen to you, toss your keys one way while you hurry off the other way. If you have children in the backseat then don't comply.

Locking your car doors isn't just about keeping somebody from stealing your car, it's about keeping you safe from harm. For instance, a few years ago my niece had an experience in a parking lot where a guy tried entering her car from the passenger side of the vehicle but, as luck would have it, she had the doors locked. When the door wouldn't open the guy quickly walked away and my niece, startled as she was, started her car and sped off.

I say she was lucky because, as she'll admit, she rarely ever locks her doors after getting inside. Who knows what that man wanted, her car, purse, or maybe her? Fortunately, we'll never know, but that scenario could have gone a quite different way if she had failed to lock her car doors that night.

Besides locking your doors, keeping the windows rolled up is a good idea as well since it's almost as easy for someone to control your actions through an open window as it is via an open door. Even just cracking the window if you must is better than rolling it all the way down when it comes to your safety.

Safety Tip # 40: Park Near Well-Lit, Busy Areas, and Move With a Purpose

Parking lot abductions, in particular, are more common than most people recognize, as this article points out: "While kidnappings like Smith's are not as common as other kinds of abductions, law enforcement officers, security consultants and missing-person researchers say attacks like hers happen more frequently than people realize. 'When you look across the country, it happens more than people think, which is unfortunate,' said J.R. Roberts, a Savannah, Ga., security consultant who helps retailers improve their security."[37]

The article continues: "'These abductions are far less common than in settings that are less scrutinized, less monitored,' said Ernie Allen, president of the National Center for Missing and Exploited Children. 'More people are abducted on city streets than they are in parking lots of malls or stores.'"

With that in mind, whenever you have a choice, always choose to park as close to a well-lit area as you can, and the closer to the building you intend to enter the better. Even if you must circle the lot for a minute or two waiting for a spot to open, it's assuredly safer to park where there's plenty of light and closer to your intended entrance than not. Also, avoid parking near the back of the lot, if possible.

This isn't about being lazy, not at all. It's about having potential witnesses nearby should something happen. So, don't worry too much about an unlikely door ding or what your Fitbit says, you're safest as close to the storefront as possible.

On a related note, if you know you're going to be using a shopping cart for your purchases, such as during a big grocery store trip, try to park near a well-lit cart return so that you don't have very far to walk when returning the cart after you're finished loading grocery bags. Or just leave the grocery cart parked next to your car if you feel unsafe at night.

Plus, if you can pull through to a parking spot or, if possible, back in as doing so will make a hasty exit that much easier. And you really should make it a point to remember exactly where you parked because it's easy to get turned around and not remember after an hour or two of shopping. Write down the row number or take a photo if you must.

Last, be sure to walk with a purpose. Grab your belongings—keys, purse, bags—and get a move on to your destination or vehicle. Fumbling around with your belongings or going back to your car, for example, shows criminals that you're an easier target and offers more opportunities to do you harm.

What if You Have Small Children or a Baby With You?

Children—especially those who need help getting into and out of a car or with being buckled up— definitely slow things down and are all the more reason to ensure you park in a well-lit, busy area with plenty of people around.

Even so, you may want to take extra precaution as this website recommends: "If you have a baby with you while loading groceries into your car, position yourself so the open car door and cart surround (protect) you. Keep the baby in the cart until you finish loading the groceries. If loading into the trunk, have a convex mirror (available at auto parts stores) affixed inside your trunk lid so you can watch behind you. To load your baby into your car (after loading the groceries, the baby goes in last), get into the rear seat with your baby, lock the doors, and buckle your baby into the safety-seat. Now look around, have pepper spray in hand, get out of the rear seat and into the driver's seat, again lock the doors, and immediately drive away. Always use this routine and it'll become second nature."[38]

That's a bit more vigilance than even I would tend to recommend, but I commend their enthusiasm. Surely there's no harm in being extra cautious, especially when your children are potentially at risk.

Safety Tip # 41: Don't Pull Over When Motioned by Another Driver

Unless there's some obvious reason to pull over, such as the engine clearly smoking, never pull over when motioned to do so by another driver. I promise, your car almost surely won't explode if you don't. Besides, it will become obvious if there is a problem, so much so that you won't need somebody else to tell you; either that or you will continue to have different motorists motioning for you to pull over, in which case I would heed their warnings. If you are concerned that there is a safety problem then drive to the nearest well-lit area, such as a gas station, and check it for yourself. If you're still unsure, go get the service station attendant to look as well since there's no harm in getting a second opinion.

Of course, not all men are trying to pull a fast one on you. I remember a while back while at my local YMCA that I motioned to a lady as she pulled out of her parking spot that there was a problem with her car. When she backed up the concrete block had pulled a portion of her front bumper away and it was likely going to drag. She was hesitant to even roll the window down to see what I wanted. She finally did, and I stayed back while I told her what happened. I get her reluctance. The takeaway? Be cautious no matter where you are, how many people are around, or what time of day it is.

Safety Tip # 42: Routine Vehicle Maintenance

You can become stranded for reasons besides running out of gas. While some scenarios are unavoidable, there's no reason to make a breakdown more likely by ignoring your vehicle's occasional maintenance needs. I'm talking about the basics here, like getting your oil changed, keeping the tires inflated—including the spare tire which most people forget—and ensuring the battery is in good working order, to name a few of the obvious maintenance needs every vehicle requires. Nearly any auto repair shop can and will perform maintenance tasks like these for a relatively minimal fee.

Remember, too, that keeping your vehicle in good working order isn't just about avoiding an unwanted breakdown. Here's a few thoughts as to why:

- Ignoring bald tires could cause your vehicle to be unable to stop or not allow you to swerve out of the way of an otherwise avoidable accident that *you* may now be at fault for.
- A dead battery won't keep the hazard lights flashing which means approaching cars may not see your stranded vehicle on the side of the road and, thus, cause a rear-end collision.
- A dead battery also won't be able to recharge your phone if you need to call for help.

- Failing to change the engine oil can make acceleration sluggish which, in the wrong circumstances, could result in an accident that would then be your fault.
- Low engine coolant could cause the engine to overheat, thus stranding you and others in severe summer heat or bitter winter weather.
- Bad windshield wipers reduce visibility and may cause you to not see a stopped vehicle ahead or a pedestrian crossing the street.
- A non-functioning headlight or brake light may cause other drivers to not see you in time and, thus, cause an accident. Or you may be stopped by the police unnecessarily which is never fun.

I hope you understand why keeping your vehicle in working order is so important by now. These simple, routine maintenance tasks aren't hard to get done, usually don't cost a lot, and can save a life. Plus, they'll help to ensure you're never stranded on the side of the road when you don't absolutely have to be.

Take a moment now to understand the maintenance tasks that need to be done, write them down or add it to your phone calendar as a recurring event. That's what I do. In so doing, I'm forced to think about my vehicle's maintenance every so often even if I don't have anything specific to do. Lastly, read this article if you need a list of vehicle maintenance tasks.[39]

Safety Tip # 43: Keep the Gas Tank Half-Full

This happens to be a pet peeve of mine. I'm a stickler for keeping our vehicle gas tanks no less than half-full for emergency preparedness purposes. With regards to your personal safety, doing so ensures you're less likely to ever be stranded on the side of the road because you unexpectedly ran out of gas, as might happen after being stuck in traffic for hours on end.

In fact, not long ago my niece (the same one as before) ran out of gas and had to call my wife for help. Of course, I came along and, though it wasn't a big deal because she was relatively close to our home, what if she was a long way away? Or, what if my wife and I couldn't help at that moment? How long would it have been until help arrived? And who's to say whether a good Samaritan would've stopped to help her or someone looking for trouble. Being alone on the side of the road is no place to be if it can be avoided.

Running out of gas just isn't a situation where anyone—man or woman—should ever find themselves when it's so easy to fill up regularly. Please do yourself a favor and get into the habit of not allowing your vehicle's gas tank to routinely dip below half a tank. You're just asking for trouble or, at the very least, an inconvenience to your day that simply didn't need to occur.

Safety Tip # 44: Prepare for Breakdowns

If your vehicle does breakdown and you know you're going to be stranded for a while, ensure you have items that may be of use, including a flashlight with extra batteries, road flares, a jacket or blanket, some water, and maybe some shelf-stable snacks which should be replaced regularly. You may also want to include a pair of sneakers to walk in should the need arise; even a pair of roll up flats is better than heels.

One item I find exceptionally useful for situations where I return to the car after a long outing and have a dead battery (say, I left a dome light on) is a portable jump starter because they can be used to jump start a dead battery without need of jumper cables and can even keep your phone or other electronics charged. They're great because you can literally jump start your car in a few minutes and be on your way again. For the price you can't beat their convenience.

Although there are many options available, I recently purchased this Tacklife 800-amp Car Jump Starter for multiple vehicles of ours and I'm quite happy with it, though I would suspect that there will be even better options available as technology improves and prices drop.[40] Remember that no matter what jump starter you purchase, you'll need to periodically charge it even if unused to ensure the unit is ready when needed. Once every six months or so if unused should suffice, but I would still check it every few months.

Safety Tip # 45: If Your Car Does Break Down

Pull off the roadway as far as you can, stay inside the vehicle, lock your doors, and engage the hazard lights. Yes, this could possibly attract unwanted attention, but your obligation is to alert other vehicles of your breakdown because you're now a hazard to them.

Call for assistance. I would suggest AAA which we've had for years, but most insurance companies offer something similar. Realize that roadside assistance is something you'll need to investigate and purchase before you have a problem as most useful roadside service plans have a built-in delay before benefits kick in to keep people from waiting to join. Or you could just call any local towing company and pay a small fortune for their help. I suggest you be proactive.

If it will be some time before help arrives, consider calling a family member or friend who can stay on the line with you until help does arrive. Of course, you may instead choose to walk to a safer place, such as a gas station or other open place of business, if it's nearby and daytime. Nighttime may be a different story since you're more vulnerable walking in the dark. In any case, if there's a reason you feel unsafe while you're waiting or walking, such as someone offering to help who doesn't seem quite right, call 9-1-1 immediately and ensure this person knows you have the police on the phone.

Additional Safety Considerations While Driving

Safety Tip # 46: Have Your Car Keys Out and Ready

Get your keys out and ready to use before leaving the house or store, for example, instead of digging for them in your purse as you approach your vehicle. This is a perfect ambush time as you'll be clearly distracted looking for your keys, and criminals know that.

Safety Tip # 47: If You Get a Flat Tire in the Parking Lot

If you have a flat tire or the car won't start upon returning to your vehicle after a shopping trip, for example, immediately return to the store you came from and call for help from there rather than waiting in your vehicle.

Safety Tip # 48: Don't Look Under Your Vehicle Before Approaching, Look to the Sides Instead

There's actually no need to look under your vehicle if it has a tall profile as with an SUV or large truck to ensure nobody is hiding underneath as this Snopes article points out.[41] This potential threat is far less of a concern than most folks believe. Most small cars and minivans aren't a problem either because adults simply cannot fit underneath. Passenger vans parked next to your driver's door also aren't a concern as this Snopes article suggests.[42] What's a bigger concern? Somebody crouched next to or behind a vehicle, even a small one, nearby. Keep your eyes up, not down.

Safety Tip # 49: Be Wary of Strangers Asking for Help

Be cautious of any stranger asking you for anything or offering to help, even women. They're more than likely a well-meaning individual, but you never know. Keep your distance and your head up. If you don't truly feel comfortable, politely decline their request. They'll get over it. Last, don't pick up hitchhikers, even a lone woman because they can be dangerous too.

Safety Tip # 50: Don't Keep Your Purse on the Seat

Keep your purse out of view on the floor, especially when you're preoccupied such as when filling up at the gas station, and even while driving, but not under your feet to keep the pedals unobstructed. Better yet, secure your purse straps through the driver's seat belt strap. Doing so will not only make it difficult to smash and grab but will also keep it from flying around and possibly injuring you or others during an accident.

Safety Tip # 51: If You're Afraid of Being Followed

If you are worried you're being followed while driving, lock your doors and roll up the windows, then just keep going until you get somewhere that's clearly busy with other people, like a gas station or grocery store. Making consecutive turns to lose them probably won't work and pulling over in a bid to let them pass could cause you to get blocked in with nowhere to go. If all else fails, call the police while you're driving if it's obvious you're being followed.

Safety Tip # 52: Check Mirrors Regularly When Driving

Check your mirrors frequently, even when stopped at a light. You'll be more aware if somebody may be sneaking up on your blind spot or following you. In addition, consider adding blind spot mirrors to your side view mirrors to make spotting trouble easier.

Safety Tip # 53: Consider Wearing a Ballcap

Think about wearing a hoodie or ballcap or something similar while driving at night to appear male to other drivers. This could have the added benefit of appearing to be a male while walking to and from your car in a parking lot, though it may obscure your peripheral vision as well.

Safety Tip # 54: Only Give Out Your Car Key

Only give a mechanic or valet the vehicle car key since a house key can be easily duplicated with a key cutting machine. Or use a valet key if you have one.

Safety Tip # 55: Add an Emergency Escape Tool

You might want to add a keychain Emergency Escape Tool.[43] It can be used to cut a stuck seat belt or break door window glass. Get a brightly colored one (not black or other dull color) so that it can be easily seen and attach it to your keychain or, better yet, to your seat belt or purse instead. That way it should always be within arm's reach because items, including keys, can become dislodged and lost in an accident.

Safety While Driving Takeaways

Here, again, your safety while driving and around vehicles is really about routines, like having your keys out as you walk to your car, coupled with a healthy dose of skepticism, such as being motioned to pull over when nothing clearly seems wrong. My advice: trust your gut. If something doesn't feel right to you, back off, seek help, and be sure the situation is safe. Here's what else you need to remember:

- Lock your doors as soon as you get in or out of your vehicle and be sure to park near well-lit areas so you can see others and they can see you—the witnesses, not so much the criminals.

- Keep your vehicle in good working order and don't let the gas tank hover around empty, ever. Your personal safety aside, there's no reason to put yourself in a bad spot when you don't have to be, particularly when due to a preventable breakdown.

- If something doesn't look or feel right when approaching your vehicle, like you got a flat tire or an odd stranger is asking for help, return to the store and seek assistance.

- Your purse and other bags are a magnet for criminals. Keep them out of sight.

- Although not mentioned previously, I would encourage you to keep an extra $20-40 for gas stashed in your car in case your purse gets lost.

Safety While Shopping

Figure 5

Shopping is a favorite and enjoyable activity for many, but it doesn't come without some risk to your personal safety. Consider the following.

Safety Tip # 56: Ask for an Escort to Your Vehicle

Ask for an escort at night when returning to your car from a shopping trip if you had to park a long distance away, like in the back of the parking lot, or if you otherwise feel unsafe. Most stores will be happy to assist you. If you feel silly asking for help *because* you're feeling unsafe—you shouldn't—simply ask them to help you to your car with your bags because you have a bum knee or whatever excuse you prefer.

Safety Tip # 57: Be Cautious When Opening Your Purse

Be wary of who's around when opening your purse as exposing your driver's license or credit cards even momentarily can cause them to become compromised by criminals in any number of ways including via RFID card readers or hidden cameras.

In addition, avoid making large payments, particularly with cash, for expensive items when others are around as some criminals will purposefully frequent well-to-do establishments looking for people they can follow to their cars or home. Just be discreet about it.

Safety Tip # 58: Never Turn Your Back on Your Purse

I can't tell you how many times I've seen women in the grocery store leave their purse unattended as they peruse the aisles, completely unaware of someone nearby. I'm surprised more purses aren't stolen as a result. I suggest you wear your purse or, at least always keep your hand on it while browsing.

Safety Tip # 59: Don't Carry Money in Bank Envelopes

Don't carry cash in bank envelopes as they're easily recognizable. Take the money out and dispose of the envelope promptly because even an empty bank envelope in your vehicle suggests you're an easy cash score if a thief is scoping out vehicles in a parking lot.

Safety Tip # 60: If Asked for Your Address

If asked for your home address or phone number while checking in or out of a hotel or at the pharmacist, for instance, and there are other people nearby, consider writing down your address on a piece of paper or handing over your driver's license so as not to broadcast such personal information aloud.

Safety Tip # 61: Protect Your Belongings When Dining

When dining out, keep important belongings like your purse and shopping bags out of sight under the table preferably between your feet or, better yet, placed directly on your lap. You could even go so far as to loop a foot or arm through one of the purse straps for added peace of mind. Of course, you'll want to ensure the purse stays zipped shut to avoid someone quickly reaching inside while you're distracted.

Safety Tip # 62: Restrooms and Narrow Corridors

Avoid clearly unfrequented restrooms or corridors anywhere you might find them—especially at night—such as at restaurants, shopping malls, and stadiums. For some reason they always seem to attract unsavory people. Better yet, try to use a family restroom even if you don't have small children as they're also often more accessible to the public and, therefore, visible.

Safety Tip # 63: Be Wary of Survey Takers

Avoid answering surveys that are not clearly setup outside of well-established businesses such as the grocery store or Walmart. Even people walking around in the parking lot with a clipboard should be considered suspect as they could quickly fake a petition for whatever heart-bleeding cause of the day is and very easily get your home address or phone number. In fact, most people would happily fill out almost any questionnaire if their emotions have temporarily blinded them.

Safety While Shopping Takeaways

Fortunately, much of what will keep you safe while shopping has already been discussed previously, including keeping your awareness, parking near well-lit areas, and having your keys out and ready to use. Here's what else you need to remember:

- If you ever feel unsafe returning to your vehicle, ask for an escort. Most establishments would be more than happy to provide one.
- Pay extra special attention to your purse and belongings as they make easy targets for criminals, including while eating out.
- Be cautious when opening your purse or providing personal information to store clerks as criminals could be paying attention. Write down such information, if possible.

Safety When Out for the Night

Figure 6

Going out for the night is often a lot of fun, especially the younger you are. Most of the time everything works out great and there's no problem whatsoever, which is how it should be. But other times you might run into a difficult situation. Fortunately, you can make such situations less likely by doing a few things differently, but you may need a bit of a mindset change to make that happen, especially with leaving a purse at home if you're accustomed to taking one.

Aside from a shift in mindset, most of the remaining advice given here should be common sense to most folks, but we'll cover them just to be sure.

Safety Tip # 64: Leave Your Purse at Home

I remember my grandmother's purse; it was so large that I swear she kept the kitchen sink in there. And that's to say nothing for extra pairs of glasses, a huge coin purse, assorted medications, and plenty more. What else? I'm afraid to ask, and there's often no reason to carry so much stuff any longer. In fact, these days many women are opting to take less with them, and maybe you should too. You might even be able to get away with leaving your purse at home altogether.

After all, there are alternatives that may be just as useful such as a small backpack if you simply must carry more. Using a backpack would leave your hands free for other tasks—including self-defense—and is probably easier on your shoulders and arms too.

That said, you might be able to do with taking less to begin with. For instance, my wife uses a Franklin Day Planner and has for many years. It's works fine for her purposes. My niece uses a smartphone case that carries her phone, credit cards, and other important cards and nothing else. I assume lipstick and the like go in her pocket or stay in the car. Even better, try a Sport2People Running Pouch Belt which stays hidden under your clothing for added security.[44]

If you must take a purse with you, don't leave it unattended in plain sight in your vehicle even if the doors are locked. The same can be said for any bags or backpacks that look like they may hold something to steal as criminals will smash and grab anything that looks valuable, even if you're only going to be gone for a few minutes. As an example, a few years ago we had friends have a backpack stolen from the cab of their truck simply because it was seen from the outside when walking by. Even though there was no indication what was inside the backpack, someone chose to break in and take it on the off chance there was something useful. Thieves really are that brazen.

If you do take a purse while shopping at a grocery store, for instance, keep it closed and never leave it unsecured in your cart. If you prefer not to carry the bag on your person, consider wrapping the purse strap around the cart handle a few times and then use a carabiner to secure your purse strap to itself so that it cannot be easily snatched. Even then, the entire cart could be taken, so keep your hand on the cart while you shop.

Although I specifically discuss purses here, the same can be said for any large bags that you must carry. Now, I understand that if you have young children then you're likely going to need a hefty diaper bag and who knows what else. In this case, I would encourage you to do your best to consolidate the bags you take with you when leaving the house. Doing so will surely make your life just a bit easier when you're already loaded down enough.

Safety Tip # 65: If They Only Want Your Purse

If an attacker appears to only be after your purse or shopping bags, let them have it because material items can all be replaced, you cannot be. If possible, throw whatever they're after in one direction while you run the other way. If you're worried about them discovering your home address or other personal information, odds are that they're only interested in your money and prescription pills. In fact, your purse will probably be found rummaged through a few blocks away. In any case, cancel your credit and debit card as soon as possible.

What if they have a weapon, particularly a knife or a gun pointed at you? Here, again, the odds are that they only want your purse, car keys or bags. In any case, you still want to avoid contact with your assailant. As such, if tossing your purse or keys in one direction while you run in the other feels like a bad idea, then drop whatever they're after on the ground and run off because the weapon they're wielding is most likely only for intimidation purposes.

Besides, in the relatively unlikely event that they did choose to shoot at you, know that even the police don't hit their target most of the time due to stress and, even then, usually miss vital organs. I know it sounds scary, but that's what the statistics reveal.

Safety Tip # 66: Reconsider Your Attire

I recognize that women like to dress up when going out, often wearing dresses or skirts, high heels, and fancy jewelry, such as necklaces and bracelets. Unfortunately, most women's outfits and accessories make it significantly more difficult to run away or fight off an assailant. Four-inch heels may look good, but they're useless—even detrimental—when it comes to your personal safety. The same goes for most everything else women like to wear when out for a night on the town.

To make matters worse, some items like necklaces or scarves can make it even easier for an assailant to grab hold of you when they otherwise might not be able to. Moreover, most clothing for outings make it difficult to carry or hide pepper spray or other personal self-defense tools. Perhaps the only option is to carry a small crossbody purse, but then your defensive tool of choice may get buried inside.

There's something to be said for frequenting the wrong establishments or being out late. I like to tell my oldest—now adult—child that "nothing good ever happens after midnight," and I continue to stand by that statement. Men are usually more intoxicated, tired, and perhaps even frustrated if they've been shot down by women throughout the night. None of these truisms make men kinder or more considerate, only more aggressive, and inappropriate.

Safety Tip # 67: Courtesy Car Drivers

Although assaults by courtesy car drivers are relatively rare, there's no reason not to be vigilant when interacting with them. Here are some thoughts:

- When requesting a ride, do so from inside the establishment you're requesting a ride from, if possible. Only go outside once your driver has arrived as indicated from within the app.
- Check that the car, license plate, and driver are who you expect to see as many vehicles look remarkably similar. If something doesn't match, request a new ride no matter what the driver says. You may even want to take a photo of the license plate for later reference.
- Have the driver confirm by name who they're here to pick up and confirm their name before entering the vehicle.
- Always ride in the back and stay awake.
- Share your ride information with trusted family or a friend as there's now usually an option from inside the app to do so easily.
- Track the ride yourself via a GPS tracker like Google Maps to ensure you're going where you expect to be.
- Trust your instincts. If something feels wrong, say so. Call the authorities if you must.
- Upon arrival, ask the driver to wait until you get inside if you feel unsafe.

Additional Safety Considerations When Out for the Night

Safety Tip # 68: Use a Crossbody Purse or Bag

Wearing a purse or bag with a strap long enough to sling over one should and worn across your body is more difficult to quickly remove. At the very least, a criminal will have to be more determined to take it. Search Amazon for *anti-theft purse* or *anti-theft bag* and you'll find plenty of options. I would suggest you look for a smaller profile design so that you're unencumbered as much as possible; they're sometimes referred to as a *crossbody wallet*.

Safety Tip # 69: There's Safety in Numbers

Everyone knows that there is safety in numbers. Groups of three or more is great, but even having one other friend is better than being by yourself. Granted, being safer together does no good unless everyone abides by the expectation to stick together which means you shouldn't let friends go off on their own.

Safety Tip # 70: Be an Aware and Vocal Friend

Women can usually spot a creep, especially when their friends seem to be unable to. Trust your gut and don't be afraid to speak up when friends are making a mistake with the wrong guy. If it was meant to be then the guy will understand. Plus, there's no harm in taking things slowly.

Safety Tip # 71: Social Media Don'ts

Don't check in or post on social media (e.g., Facebook, Instagram, TikTok) where you are. Social media accounts can be easily followed by unknown people on some social sites if you don't set them up properly. And considering how important it is for young people to *have the most* followers these days, it's all too easy to let the creeps in as well.

Safety Tip # 72: Pour Your Own Drinks

Pour your own drinks at house parties, watch the bartender do it when at a bar or nightclub, and never let someone you just met fetch your drinks for you unless it's the waiter or waitress. Know that ordering mixed drinks can be further problematic because they take longer to make and thus allow more opportunity for someone to slip in a roofie without you realizing.

Please don't underestimate just how easy this. Friends of ours recounted a story to us not long ago of someone they know who had this very scenario happen to her. That is, some sort of muscle relaxer was used to make it so that she was capable enough to walk out of a place on her own—initially, anyway— but was then unable to stop what occurred later. I don't know whether the guy was caught or not, but I'm willing to bet this young lady strongly regrets not having taken this very real concern more seriously.

Safety Tip # 73: Tell Others Where You're Going

Tell someone where you're going for the night, with whom, and when you expect to be back. In my opinion, there's no harm in sharing your location via a smartphone GPS tracker with a trusted family member or friend. We use Life360 and the free version works well. Granted, they're not always precise down to the exact house address, but they are usually accurate enough so that it's obvious if somebody is where they're expected to be or not.

Safety Tip # 74: Never Allow Yourself to be Moved

If you are assaulted and unable to flee, never let the assailant move you to another location as the odds of the encounter getting worse for you skyrocket drastically. Scream, kick, bite, and do anything you can to be too much trouble in the eyes of the attacker. This scenario, I'm afraid, may be the one time where a weapon is more likely to be used against you if it's been shown up front because the assailant already has worse plans in mind now that you're actively resisting.

Safety Tip # 75: Avoid Confined Places

Avoid being alone in secluded places such as stairwells, alleyways, and even hallways of questionable establishments. It's only common sense according to every scary teen horror movie ever made, right? Elevators are better, but still not great.

Safety Tip # 76: Showing Kindness to Strangers

Criminals sometimes prey on the kindness of women. If somebody asks for directions or for the time, for instance, be courteous and helpful if that's your nature but keep your distance, nonetheless. Of course, never follow someone elsewhere because you've been asked to. You don't need to be polite in saying you're not going anywhere because you don't feel it's safe.

Safety Tip # 77: Getting into an Unknown Vehicle

Never get into an assailant's vehicle, ever. Run away as fast as you can. If running away doesn't seem possible, run around a parked car like the song "Ring Around the Rosie" until they give up. If even that doesn't seem like it will work, try getting under a parked vehicle with your back to the ground and hold on to anything you can. Remember that getting under most sedans or minivans won't work since their profiles are exceptionally low to the ground.

Safety Tip # 78: Late Night Working Hours

Although not related to going out on the town, avoid being the closer at work if the establishment is typically open late. If you must close, be sure someone else is there with you until you both exit and get into your respective vehicles.

Safety While Out for the Night Takeaways

Going out with friends for the night is always fun, but you need to consider your safety too, and that starts before you even leave your home. Avoid posting where you're headed on social platforms, reconsider your dress, and think about leaving items that will encumber your movements at home, specifically the purse and high heel shoes. Here's what else you need to remember:

- Friends are your greatest ally to keep from making any number of mistakes that night. Listen to them if they have a bad feeling about a guy since their gut is probably right.
- Always tell a trusted family member or friend where you're headed for the night, even if it's only via a mobile app such as Life360.
- Women are usually kind and helpful, but that kindness can get you into trouble if you're unable to say no when needed.
- Never allow yourself to be put into an assailant's vehicle or to be moved from your current location. The odds of the encounter getting worse for you escalate dramatically.
- If you must take a purse, use a smaller profile crossbody purse or wallet. They're more difficult to steal and will force you to take fewer items which means you'll be less encumbered should you need to be.

Safety When Traveling

Figure 7

Traveling the country—even abroad—is so easy to do these days and generally a lot of fun, often creating lifetime memories. But it's also a prime time for criminals to target unsuspecting vacationers because they're either unaware of their newfound surroundings or preoccupied with having a good time, which means you really do need to be extra vigilant.

That said, I know women who travel alone without trouble, some of whom travel overseas by themselves too. The important part to realize is that they're very on top of their travel plans, ensuring they know all the details of their itinerary, and cautious about what and with whom they share their information.

Safety Tip # 79: Reduce Your Luggage Load

Most of the women in my life drive me a bit crazy when it comes to packing luggage for a trip. For some reason they always include way too many articles of clothing, shoes, and so much else—my mother-in-law actually packs her favorite pillows in one suitcase alone—that there's no way they could ever do anything for their own safety because there are so many suitcases in tow.

Although it usually works out for us because there are enough people to haul every last suitcase, if you're traveling on your own then I would encourage you to have only one small suitcase to handle so that you always have one hand free. Or, better yet, use a backpack instead to keep both hands free; search Amazon for *anti-theft backpack* or the Pacsafe Venturesafe backpack is a good choice.[45] Just to be safe, you should keep your money, credit cards, driver's license, and other small valuables on your person rather than in a suitcase or even a backpack.

Last, one action my mother takes when flying domestically is to ship extra items—more clothes and shoes—via UPS a week before her flight, that way she only has a small suitcase to carry. Most hotels will happily accept parcels for their guests, but you'll want to time their arrival so that the hotel isn't hanging onto a box for weeks. Realize, however, that shipping internationally may prove cost prohibitive.

Safety Tip # 80: Secure Your Valuables

Although many hotels and hostels tend to offer some sort of safe or locker that's better than nothing, you may find the need to secure your own valuables at times. An easy solution—so that it's packable in your luggage—is the Pacsafe Travelsafe.[46] Add in a TSA-approved luggage lock and you'll be well on your way to better securing your valuables from snatch and grab thieves.[47] No doubt, this idea isn't foolproof, but clearly better than nothing and easier than hauling everything around all day.

Next, ensure your most important items—phone, money, credit cards, passport—are always carried on your person. You can do so in a variety of ways such as in a visible secure storage option like a waist belt bag or an anti-theft shoulder bag or, better yet, something hidden as is the case with a hidden bra wallet or hidden money belt underneath your clothing.[48,49,50] There are plenty of options out there, so many that you should take your time finding something which works for you.

Additionally, you might want to start using something that blocks RFID signals since thieves are becoming more technologically-savvy, even in your day-to-day life. Look for something that includes RFID-blocking in the title, or you can simply purchase a set of RFID-blocking Sleeves.[51] Alternatively, these RFID-blocking Cards may be a more convenient option these days.[52]

Safety Tip # 81: Protect Your Financials

We all know bad things may still happen despite taking extra precautions. To keep a bad situation like getting your money or passport stolen from becoming worse, you'll want to take some steps to make recovery easier while you're away from home.

Make copies of your important documents, including debit or credit card phone numbers, bank contact information, and your passport if you're traveling abroad. You can then choose to leave a copy of these items with a trusted family member or friend, upload them to a secure cloud service, and even include them in more than one secure spot—such as a money belt under your clothing—while you travel. You'll also want to divvy up your resources (e.g., money, credit cards) so that if any one location is compromised then you're not completely without resources.

Here's a useful layered strategy: "I keep one credit card, my passport and a day's worth of cash in a wallet in my zippered pocket or sling handbag. Another credit card and form of identification, copies of my passport and credit cards and most of my cash are in a cotton money belt that is secure around my waist and inaccessible under my clothing." The article continues, "In a third stash, which I keep hidden inside my suitcase or backpack, is another credit card, a small amount of emergency cash and additional copies of my passport and credit cards."[53]

If it were me, I would take credit cards instead of a debit card because they're usually easier to dispute or cancel if you had to. In addition, I would choose to take two different credit cards in case one gets compromised. Use one as your primary card and keep the other unused and stashed away in your money belt. You'll also want to make sure your credit card companies know that you're traveling. Typically, they're going to contact you very quickly if they notice something unusual anyway. Of course, you'll need to ensure your phone works if travelling internationally; contact your phone carrier to be sure.

Last, check your credit card transactions regularly to keep abreast of unusual activity. In fact, many institutions now offer text or email alerts which makes it even easier without having to login each day.

Protect Your Identity

Realize that your identity is a hot resource for criminal organizations, even more so than your credit cards or debit card because it can be used to commit even bigger crimes down the road, often without your realizing it until months later and at the worst of times like trying to purchase a new car or qualify for a home loan. Take extra precautions when sharing any personally identifiable information including your home address, date of birth, and definitely your social security number, among other details you should be wary of sharing.[54]

Safety Tip # 82: Stay Off All Wi-Fi Networks

No doubt Wi-Fi is convenient, and we've all become accustomed to it, but it's also easily compromised by cyberhackers these days. Even if you have good antivirus or antimalware software on your electronics (as well as your smartphone) you may unwittingly compromise these devices in many ways, as is the case with email phishing scams or inadvertently connecting to what you thought was the hotel Wi-Fi network when it wasn't.

Before you know it, cybercriminals are stealing your bank login credentials and transferring your assets to an offshore account and you're none the wiser. Two days later they're sipping Mai Tais on a beach in the Caribbean. Ok, maybe it's not quite that easy for them to pull off, but they're smarter than most of us realize.

With that in mind, always use your cellular data for sensitive logins like bank accounts and even email and, if possible, for all online activity. Be aware, though, that doing so may cost you in data usage charges, especially if using data abroad. Also, consider a password manager tool like LastPass.com or KeeperSecurity.com.[55,56]

On a similar note, don't allow your electronics to broadcast that they're discoverable when connected to a Wi-Fi network and don't allow your phone to be discoverable via Bluetooth either.

Additional Safety Considerations for Traveling

Safety Tip # 83: Confirm Reservations Before Leaving

Confirm reservations (flights, hotels, car rentals or courtesy car drivers, etc.) shortly before leaving. Sometimes things change last-minute and you don't want to be scrambling to fix a problem at the last possible moment.

Safety Tip # 84: Avoid Wearing Jewelry

Avoid taking expensive jewelry when traveling. It just attracts attention and may make you an unnecessary target to the wrong people.

Safety Tip # 85: Luggage Tags as Source of Information

Luggage tags shouldn't include your home address or even your phone number. Use a virtual phone number instead, such as those intended for online dating safety and privacy. I believe Google Voice is still a free alternative if you need a recommendation.[57]

Safety Tip # 86: Wear a Wedding Band

Wear a remarkably simple wedding band even if you are not married; costume jewelry is a good option. Doing so may keep some creeps away since they'll assume you're not available. Clearly, it would be wise to keep your expensive wedding ring at home so that it doesn't get stolen or lost.

Safety Tip # 87: Write Down Information from Clerks

Ask the hotel receptionist to write down your room number if there are others in line to not broadcast it. The same can be said for any sensitive information you may need to share with them.

Safety Tip # 88: Avoid Lingering People, Not Just Men

Pay attention to anyone lingering in the hallways, stairways, or near the elevator. Realize that it's not just men you need to watch for, women can cause trouble as well, and even act as a lookout.

Safety Tip # 89: Hotel Door Security

Always lock your hotel door immediately upon entering if it's not automatic, and ensure the door fully closes behind you each time. It should go without saying to check through the peephole before answering the door, even if you're expecting room service, for example, to ensure whoever is on the other side is who you expect.

Safety Tip # 90: Pack Additional Door Security

Even if your hotel room door is solid with heavy locks, it never hurts to carry an Adalock and Travel Door Alarm to further secure the main hotel door.[58,59] I would even encourage you to add a Wundermax Door Stopper to better secure the bathroom door for when you're in the shower.[60]

Safety Tip # 91: If Traveling Alone

Never tell people you are traveling alone, though it will be obvious to people like hotel receptionists and courtesy car drivers. All others should be kept in the dark about this fact.

Safety Tip # 92: Review Travel Advisories

Review the State Department Travel Advisories website before you book a trip because they're pretty good at keeping tabs on whether Americans would be safe traveling to specific countries or not.[61] And, of course, review the travel advisory website shortly before leaving just in case something changed.

Safety Tip # 93: Know Local Customs and Laws

Like it or not, even some first-world countries have vastly different customs and laws than the United States. For instance, tipping a waitress in Japan or sitting in the back of a cab in Australia may be considered offensive. In an effort not to offend locals, it's a good idea to know their customs and laws. Research an appropriate website before traveling to another country so you know what to expect.

Safety Tip # 94: Avoid Being Out After Dark

Just like at home, life is always a bit more dangerous at night because the wrong people tend to come out. And, because you're less familiar with local customs, you're therefore more likely to fall victim to scams overseas. Try to keep your outings to daylight hours.

Safety Tip # 95: Know Your Itinerary Each Day

Know your itinerary for the day before leaving if you're unfamiliar with the area, especially if you're going through an organized tour because there's nothing worse than being stranded in a foreign county when you're lost and unable to speak the language. In addition, let the hotel or hostel receptionist know where you're leaving and when you expect to return because the better ones are good about keeping tabs on their guests.

Arrange all tours and transportation from the hotel or from agencies they recommend. Avoid going it alone.

Safety Tip # 96: Learn to Say Help

At the very least, learn to say help in the language of any country you visit. I would also suggest a translation app with offline capability, then download all appropriate dialects for the country you're visiting. The Google Translate app does this well.[62]

Safety Tip # 97: Money Exchanges

Exchange money at the hotel or hostel, or ask for the location of a secure ATM, for example, one that is located inside a bank and not visible from the street.

Safety While Traveling Takeaways

When traveling, it's clear that you need to be even more vigilant than normal. Criminals, especially those abroad, willfully target travelers because they know vacationers are easier marks. To be as prepared as possible and to avoid unnecessary trouble, you should have your travel plans, itinerary, and contacts lined up well in advance of your travel date, including all hotel bookings and sightseeing adventures. Here's what else you need to remember:

- Pack light because the more suitcases and bags you have the more there is to keep track of or to lose; the same can be said for the information you share with others.
- Secure your financials and valuables when traveling, including making copies of important documents before leaving, using a travel safe, and employing any number of anti-theft bags or wallets.
- Stay off Wi-Fi. Use cellular data, if possible.
- Avoid standing out by wearing expensive jewelry or appearing unmarried.
- Boost your hotel door security with additional locks and door alarms.
- Be extra cautious when traveling abroad by reviewing State Department travel advisories, knowing local customs and laws, and utilizing translation apps, to name a few.

Final Thoughts

Hopefully, most of the tips provided were common sense, though I suspect you nonetheless encountered solid advice you hadn't thought of as well. At the very least, you should consider the recommendations given herein as a reminder of what you should be doing each day or, better yet, as a jumpstart to begin doing so if you haven't been.

And while I do want you to come away from reading this feeling more prepared for the world and what you may encounter, I don't want you to come away fearful. After all, most of your experiences and interactions with others are fine and nothing to worry about. It's those very few instances, however, that are potentially problematic. Alas, it's only through practicing crucial actions such as what we've discussed throughout that will make the difference when difficult circumstances arise. Unfortunately, neither will you likely get much warning something bad is coming nor a second chance to get it right.

Therefore, it's crucial for you to heed this advice day in and day out. While you're at it, remind others you care about to do the same and everyone will be far more likely to stay safe. After all, that's the entire point of the book: to provide you with the tools and advice you need to remain safe no matter what comes your way. Take action. Stay safe.

Get Your Free Checklist Here

Before you grab your checklist, be a good friend or family member and choose to help others who could use this crucial information.

Spread the Word, Share the Knowledge

I'm willing to bet that you have family and friends who could benefit from this book as well, so please take a moment right now and quickly share a link to it on Facebook, Twitter, or Pinterest. You can easily do so here.[63]

Now, download your free, easy-to-reference 97-point safety checklist here.[64] Or, if you prefer, the entire checklist is reproduced in Appendix A for your convenience.

Discover More Books Here

If you liked what you read within then you're going to love my other survival books.[65] Here's a sampling:

- 28 Powerful Home Security Solutions[66]
- 57 Scientifically-Proven Survival Foods to Stockpile[67]
- 53 Essential Bug Out Bag Supplies[68]
- 47 Easy DIY Survival Projects[69]
- The Complete Pet Safety Action Plan[70]
- 27 Crucial Smartphone Apps for Survival[71]
- 144 Survival Uses for 10 Common Items[72]
- The Get Home Bag and Compact EDC Kit[73]

And if you would like to be among the first to know when new survival books become available, fill out this form and you'll be notified via email.[74]

Recommended for You

I want to point out one book from the above list, in particular, since you clearly understand the importance of your safety: 28 Powerful Home Security Solutions: How to Stop Burglars from Targeting Your Home and Stealing Your Valuables.

Inside, you'll discover dozens of pieces of fundamental advice you can make use of right now to deter thieves — including three crucial actions that virtually guarantee they'll move on. With insights into how they choose their targets, which factors deter thieves, as well as when and where they strike, now you'll know how to protect your home and avoid costly, even life-threatening encounters.

And you will rest assured knowing that you have all the information you need to stay protected whether you're at home or away.

Click here and discover the precise actions you need to take to protect your home and family today.[75]

Your Opinion Matters to Me

I'd love to hear your feedback about this book, especially anything I might be able to add or improve upon for future revisions. Please send me an email at rethinksurvival@gmail.com with the word "book" in the subject if you have something for me. (And be sure to include the book title so I'm not confused.)

Review This Book on Amazon

Last, I ask that you take a moment and write a review of my book on Amazon.com so that others know what to expect, particularly if you've found my advice useful.[76]

I do hope that you've enjoyed this book and that you will choose to implement my recommendations to help keep you and other women in your life safe.

I encourage you to please take a moment and download the 97-point checklist above, share this book with your friends and family using the link I provided previously, and leave a quick review on Amazon.com while you're at it.

May God bless you and your family.

Thank you for your time, Damian

Appendices

Appendix A: 97-Point Checklist

Appendix B: List of Figures

Appendix C: List of Resources

Appendix A: 97-Point Checklist

Self-Defense Facts

- Men are typically stronger and more capable in a fight than women. Don't attempt to stand toe-to-toe unless you have no other choice.
- Assailants are often fueled by substance use which makes them even more illogical and difficult to fight off. Plus, it makes self-defense more difficult for you as well.
- You do have the moral and legal right to defend yourself if threatened with harm.
- Be verbal regardless of what the attacker says as doing so draws unwanted attention which plays into their fear of getting caught.
- Your goal is always to escape. Wait for the right moment when he's distracted to strike and then run away.

Self-Defense Safety

- Safety Tip # 1: Your Awareness is Crucial (keep your head up, not down looking at your phone)
- Safety Tip # 2: Take a Self-Defense Class (contact the local YMCA or similar facility for nearby recommendations)
- Safety Tip # 3: Consider Self-Paced Instruction (I recommend the B.E.T. system)
- Safety Tip # 4: The Most Vulnerable Body Parts (groin, eyes, throat)

- Safety Tip # 5: If Grabbed Unexpectedly (this depends on how you're grabbed, read the book for details)
- Safety Tip # 6: Personal Defense Tools (I recommend pepper spray gel over other options)
- Safety Tip # 7: Safety Whistles and Alarms (don't bother)
- Safety Tip # 8: The Fight or Flight Response (know your typical response to danger; retrain the Amygdala through practice)
- Safety Tip # 9: Carry Car Keys in Your Hand (but not for self-defense purposes)
- Safety Tip # 10: Make Eye Contact, Speak Up (makes criminals aware you can identify them)
- Safety Tip # 11: Use Your Elbow (it's the strongest point of your body)
- Safety Tip # 12: If You Have Long Hair (can be used to control you)
- Safety Tip # 13: If Facing Multiple Aggressors (don't try to fight them; choose to escape only)
- Safety Tip # 14: If They're Wielding a Firearm (odds are it's for intimidation purposes only; run fast)
- Safety Tip # 15: Should You Carry a Firearm? (personal choice)
- Safety Tip # 16: Carry a Flashlight Instead (some can be useful for self-defense purposes too)

Safety at Home

- Safety Tip # 17: Lock Doors and Windows (don't make it any easier on criminals to assault you)
- Safety Tip # 18: Make It Clear Someone Appears to be Home (tv, lights on; park a car in the driveway)
- Safety Tip # 19: Make it Obvious Criminals Might Get Caught Later (surveillance cameras, alarm system)
- Safety Tip # 20: Avoiding Home Invasions (reconsider how you answer the door; beef up front door)
  - What if They Attempt Entry? (run, hide, fight)
- Safety Tip # 21: Don't Display Your Name Publicly (makes it easier to discover personal info about you)
- Safety Tip # 22: Make Noise When You're Home (keep a tv or radio on)
- Safety Tip # 23: Moving Bags Into Your Home (lock the door behind you each time)
- Safety Tip # 24: Keep Trees and Bushes Trimmed (these make for easy hiding spots)
- Safety Tip # 25: Install Motion Sensing Lights (not only around front porch and driveway)
- Safety Tip # 26: Keep Your Distance With Deliveries

- Safety Tip # 27: If You Lose Your House Keys (replace the locks ASAP; criminals know time is of the essence)
- Safety Tip # 28: When Moving Into a New Rental (check for hidden cameras; replace exterior door locks)

Safety Around the Neighborhood

- Safety Tip # 29: Stay Off Your Phone When Out (distracts you from everything, including assailants)
- Safety Tip # 30: Walk With Someone Else (safety in numbers and something to look forward to)
    - o Why Your Dog Won't Defend You (they expect you to protect them as the pack leader)
- Safety Tip # 31: Switch Up Routines Regularly (keeps others from anticipating your movements)
- Safety Tip # 32: Use Smartphone Safety Apps (Noonlight, Life360, Watch Over Me)
- Safety Tip # 33: Ensure the Phone Battery is Charged (at least 50% or more)
- Safety Tip # 34: Avoid Wearing Earbuds When Walking (can't hear people or vehicles approaching)
- Safety Tip # 35: If You're Approached or Followed (stop, wait, change directions)

- Safety Tip # 36: Minimizing Discovery of Your Home (continue walking past or stop well short, wait)
- Safety Tip # 37: Let Family or Friends Know You're Out (ensures someone is watching over you)
- Safety Tip # 38: Avoid Potential Ambush Locations (along sides of roadways, like dense bushes)

Safety While Driving and Around Vehicles

- Safety Tip # 39: Lock Car Doors Immediately (assailants act quick and strike from your blind spot)
- Safety Tip # 40: Park Near Well-Lit, Busy Areas, and Move With a Purpose (eyewitnesses)
  - What if You Have Small Children or a Baby With You?
- Safety Tip # 41: Don't Pull Over When Motioned by Another Driver (it will be obvious there's a problem)
- Safety Tip # 42: Routine Vehicle Maintenance (helps to avoid many breakdown or dangerous scenarios)
- Safety Tip # 43: Keep the Gas Tank Half-Full (no reason to be stranded when you don't have to be)

- Safety Tip # 44: Prepare for Breakdowns (add jump starter, shoes, flashlight, water, blanket, etc.)
- Safety Tip # 45: If Your Car Does Break Down (pull off roadway; call AAA or similar; lock doors)
- Safety Tip # 46: Have Your Car Keys Out and Ready (keeps your focus up instead of down in your purse)
- Safety Tip # 47: If You Get a Flat Tire in the Parking Lot (return to store immediately and seek assistance)
- Safety Tip # 48: Don't Look Under Your Vehicle Before Approaching, Look to the Sides Instead
- Safety Tip # 49: Be Wary of Strangers Asking for Help (could be a ruse; return to store and seek help)
- Safety Tip # 50: Don't Keep Your Purse on the Seat (easier to grab or be seen by criminals)
- Safety Tip # 51: If You're Afraid of Being Followed (pull off to side of road and wait)
- Safety Tip # 52: Check Mirrors Regularly When Driving (look for blind spot ambush at signal lights, etc.)
- Safety Tip # 53: Consider Wearing a Ballcap (gives impression of being male)
- Safety Tip # 54: Only Give Out Your Car Key (don't hand out house key as they are easily duplicated)

- Safety Tip # 55: Add an Emergency Escape Tool (used to cut seat belt or break window)

Safety While Shopping

- Safety Tip # 56: Ask for an Escort to Your Vehicle (especially at night)
- Safety Tip # 57: Be Cautious When Opening Your Purse (credit cards and more can be compromised with hidden cameras and RFID-stealing equipment)
- Safety Tip # 58: Never Turn Your Back on Your Purse (too easy to snatch or reach into while distracted)
- Safety Tip # 59: Don't Carry Money in Bank Envelopes (makes it obvious you have money to steal)
- Safety Tip # 60: If Asked for Your Address (write it down or hand over driver's license)
- Safety Tip # 61: Protect Your Belongings When Dining (keep belongs between your feet or on your lap)
- Safety Tip # 62: Restrooms and Narrow Corridors (tend to attract sketchy people)
- Safety Tip # 63: Be Wary of Survey Takers (especially those roaming parking lots; could easily be fake)

Safety When Out for the Night

- Safety Tip # 64: Leave Your Purse at Home (one less item you must be concerned with)
- Safety Tip # 65: If They Only Want Your Purse (toss it one way, you run the other)
- Safety Tip # 66: Reconsider Your Attire (high heels, tight dresses, and the like make movement and, therefore, self-defense more difficult)
- Safety Tip # 67: Courtesy Car Drivers (several things to know; read the book)
- Safety Tip # 68: Use a Crossbody Purse or Bag (more secure option)
- Safety Tip # 69: There's Safety in Numbers (groups of three or more)
- Safety Tip # 70: Be an Aware and Vocal Friend (trust your gut; listen to your friends)
- Safety Tip # 71: Social Media Don'ts (don't post where you're going as it's too easy for creeps to follow your social media accounts)
- Safety Tip # 72: Pour Your Own Drinks (too easy to slip drugs into otherwise)
- Safety Tip # 73: Tell Others Where You're Going (at least via GPS tracker app)
- Safety Tip # 74: Never Allow Yourself to be Moved (odds of escalation increase dramatically)
- Safety Tip # 75: Avoid Confined Places (e.g., stairwells, alleyways)

- Safety Tip # 76: Showing Kindness to Strangers (ok to do, but keep your distance and never go elsewhere if asked to do so)
- Safety Tip # 77: Getting into an Unknown Vehicle (run away or around a vehicle until they give up)
- Safety Tip # 78: Late Night Working Hours (don't be the closer)

Safety When Traveling

- Safety Tip # 79: Reduce Your Luggage Load (take one small suitcase or backpack; ship the rest)
- Safety Tip # 80: Secure Your Valuables (use a travel safe, TSA-approved luggage lock, anti-theft bag, bra wallet, money belt, RFID-blocking sleeve, and RFID-blocking cards)
- Safety Tip # 81: Protect Your Financials and Identity (make copies of important documents, have backup credit card, check activity regularly, etc.)
- Safety Tip # 82: Stay Off All Wi-Fi Networks (easy way for hackers to steal your identity and more; use cellular data if possible)
- Safety Tip # 83: Confirm Reservations Before Leaving
- Safety Tip # 84: Avoid Wearing Jewelry (makes you a target)
- Safety Tip # 85: Luggage Tags as Source of Information (use a forwarding phone service; don't include address)

- Safety Tip # 86: Wear a Wedding Band (e.g., costume jewelry; makes you less of a target if assumed to be married)
- Safety Tip # 87: Write Down Information from Clerks (e.g., hotel room number to avoid broadcasting to others)
- Safety Tip # 88: Avoid Lingering People, Not Just Men (even women can be dangerous or lookouts)
- Safety Tip # 89: Hotel Door Security
- Safety Tip # 90: Pack Additional Door Security (bring an extra door lock, door alarm, and door stopper)
- Safety Tip # 91: If Traveling Alone (avoid telling people you're traveling alone)
- Safety Tip # 92: Review Travel Advisories (when traveling abroad for most recent advice)
- Safety Tip # 93: Know Local Customs and Laws (to avoid inadvertently insulting others)
- Safety Tip # 94: Avoid Being Out After Dark (situations are always more dangerous at night)
- Safety Tip # 95: Know Your Itinerary Each Day (so you know if something is out of place)
- Safety Tip # 96: Learn to Say Help (in the native language; download an offline translation app)
- Safety Tip # 97: Money Exchanges (be wary of where you exchange money; ask hostel for guidance)

Appendix B: List of Figures

Figure 1

Title, Description: None.
Author: klimkin (https://pixabay.com/users/klimkin-1297145/).
Image Source: https://pixabay.com/photos/karate-sunset-fight-sports-2578819/.
License: https://pixabay.com/service/license/.
Modifications: No changes were made to this image.

Figure 2

Title, Description: None.
Author: silviarita (https://pixabay.com/users/silviarita-3142410/)
Image Source: https://pixabay.com/photos/young-woman-girl-concerns-rest-2239269/.
License: https://pixabay.com/service/license/.
Modifications: No changes were made to this image.

Figure 3

Title, Description: None.
Author: Free-Photos (https://pixabay.com/users/Free-Photos-242387/)
Image Source: https://pixabay.com/photos/condominium-condo-architecture-690086/.
License: https://pixabay.com/service/license/.
Modifications: No changes were made to this image.

Figure 4

Title, Description: Blonde-haired Woman in Yellow T-shirt Wearing Black Sunglasses Holding Silver Smartphone.
Author: Andrea Piacquadio
(https://www.pexels.com/@olly)
Image Source:
https://www.pexels.com/photo/blonde-haired-woman-in-yellow-t-shirt-wearing-black-sunglasses-holding-silver-smartphone-787478/.
License: https://www.pexels.com/license/.
Modifications: No changes were made to this image.

Figure 5

Title, Description: None.
Author: gonghuimin468
(https://pixabay.com/users/gonghuimin468-3804290/)
Image Source: https://pixabay.com/photos/woman-shopping-lifestyle-beautiful-3040029/.
License: https://pixabay.com/service/license/.
Modifications: No changes were made to this image.

Figure 6

Title, Description: None.
Author: nastya_gepp
(https://pixabay.com/users/nastya_gepp-3773230/)
Image Source: https://pixabay.com/photos/three-blonde-hair-glitter-glamour-3075751/.

Figure 7

Appendix C: List of Resources

- Link 1: https://rethinksurvival.com/books/women-safety-checklist.php
- Link 2: https://rethinksurvival.com/kindle-books/
- Link 3: https://en.wikipedia.org/wiki/Average_human_height_by_country
- Link 4: https://en.wikipedia.org/wiki/Human_body_weight
- Link 5: https://www.livestrong.com/article/246036-how-much-more-muscle-mass-does-a-male-have-than-a-female/
- Link 6: https://www.verywellhealth.com/what-is-testosterone-why-is-it-important-1960146
- Link 7: https://www.psychologytoday.com/us/blog/media-spotlight/201803/how-are-substance-abuse-and-violence-related
- Link 8: https://issuesiface.com/magazine/top-10-safety-tips-for-women
- Link 9: https://www.livescience.com/36929-safety-self-defense-tips-women.html

- Link 10: https://www.livescience.com/36929-safety-self-defense-tips-women.html
- Link 11: https://coachdavidalexander.wordpress.com/b-e-t-self-defense-system/
- Link 12: https://www.udemy.com/course/self-defense-made-real-easy/
- Link 13: https://rethinksurvival.com/video-vault/personal-defense-and-firearms-videos/
- Link 14: https://www.youtube.com/watch?v=7XI1uAdr_s4
- Link 15: https://www.youtube.com/watch?v=fji463dsZXo
- Link 16: https://rethinksurvival.com/kindle-books/women-safety-recommends/#pepperspray
- Link 17: https://www.pepper-spray-store.com/pages/all-pepper-spray-state-laws
- Link 18: https://survivalfreedom.com/can-you-store-pepper-spray-in-a-car/
- Link 19: https://rethinksurvival.com/kindle-books/women-safety-recommends/#keychainwhistle
- Link 20: https://www.thenonprofits.com/safety.htm

- Link 21:
  https://blog.gunassociation.org/running-
  zigzag-pattern-actually-effective/
- Link 22: https://rethinksurvival.com/kindle-
  books/women-safety-
  recommends/#wowflashlight
- Link 23:
  https://www.youtube.com/watch?v=mcdya
  wIKXps
- Link 24: https://eyewitness.tech/americans-
  dont-lock-doors-survey/
- Link 25:
  https://www.vectorsecurity.com/blog/airef-
  study-highlights
- Link 26:
  https://www.theguardian.com/business/2017
  /aug/18/former-burglars-barking-dogs-cctv-
  best-deterrent
- Link 27:
  https://www.thehomesecuritysuperstore.co
  m/blogs/the-home-security-superstore-
  blog/astonishing-reasons-why-home-
  invasions-seem-to-be-rising
- Link 28:
  https://www.youtube.com/watch?v=Ixcqvk5
  oCrU
- Link 29:
  https://www.npr.org/sections/thetwo-
  way/2018/02/28/589453431/pedestrian-

fatalities-remain-at-25-year-high-for-second-year-in-a-row
- Link 30: https://www.newson6.com/story/5e3646172f69d76f62060542/would-your-dog-protect-you-from-an-intruder
- Link 31: https://www.noonlight.com/
- Link 32: https://www.life360.com/
- Link 33: https://watchovermeapp.com/
- Link 34: https://newsroom.aaa.com/2016/09/americans-spend-average-17600-minutes-driving-year/
- Link 35: https://www.lawfirms.com/resources/criminal-defense/violent-crime/car-jacking-statistics.htm
- Link 36: https://www.fox6now.com/news/it-happened-so-fast-61-year-old-woman-recounts-scary-wauwatosa-speedway-carjacking
- Link 37: https://bismarcktribune.com/news/state-and-regional/parking-lot-abductions-aren-t-rare/article_b345eb3b-6039-5774-8ff7-356af73e4a07.html
- Link 38: https://www.crime-safety-security.com/Parking-Lot-Safety.html

- Link 39:
  https://www.cargurus.com/Cars/articles/the
  _car_maintenance_schedule_you_should_fo
  llow
- Link 40: https://rethinksurvival.com/kindle-
  books/women-safety-
  recommends/#jumpstarter
- Link 41: https://www.snopes.com/fact-
  check/the-unkindest-cut/
- Link 42: https://www.snopes.com/fact-
  check/rape-attempt-in-vacaville/
- Link 43: https://rethinksurvival.com/kindle-
  books/women-safety-
  recommends/#escapetool
- Link 44: https://rethinksurvival.com/kindle-
  books/women-safety-
  recommends/#runningbelt
- Link 45: https://rethinksurvival.com/kindle-
  books/women-safety-
  recommends/#venturesafe
- Link 46: https://rethinksurvival.com/kindle-
  books/women-safety-recommends/#pacsafe
- Link 47: https://rethinksurvival.com/kindle-
  books/women-safety-recommends/#tsalock
- Link 48: https://rethinksurvival.com/kindle-
  books/women-safety-
  recommends/#antitheftbag
- Link 49: https://rethinksurvival.com/kindle-
  books/women-safety-
  recommends/#brawallet

- Link 50: https://rethinksurvival.com/kindle-books/women-safety-recommends/#moneywallet
- Link 51: https://rethinksurvival.com/kindle-books/women-safety-recommends/#rfidsleeve
- Link 52: https://rethinksurvival.com/kindle-books/women-safety-recommends/#rfidcard
- Link 53: https://www.bankrate.com/finance/credit-cards/female-solo-travel-guide/
- Link 54: https://www.makeuseof.com/tag/the-10-pieces-of-information-identity-thieves-are-looking-for/
- Link 55: https://www.lastpass.com/
- Link 56: https://www.keepersecurity.com/
- Link 57: https://voice.google.com/u/0/signup
- Link 58: https://rethinksurvival.com/kindle-books/women-safety-recommends/#adalock
- Link 59: https://rethinksurvival.com/kindle-books/women-safety-recommends/#dooralarm
- Link 60: https://rethinksurvival.com/kindle-books/women-safety-recommends/#doorstopper
- Link 61: https://travel.state.gov/content/travel/en/traveladvisories/traveladvisories.html/

- Link 62:
  https://play.google.com/store/apps/details?id=com.google.android.apps.translate&hl=en
- Link 63:
  https://rethinksurvival.com/books/women-safety-share.html
- Link 64:
  https://rethinksurvival.com/lp/women-safety-checklist.html
- Link 65: https://rethinksurvival.com/kindle-books/
- Link 66: https://rethinksurvival.com/kindle-books/home-security-book/
- Link 67: https://rethinksurvival.com/kindle-books/survival-foods-book/
- Link 68: https://rethinksurvival.com/kindle-books/bug-out-bag-book-v2/
- Link 69: https://rethinksurvival.com/kindle-books/diy-survival-projects-book/
- Link 70: https://rethinksurvival.com/kindle-books/pet-safety-plan-book/
- Link 71: https://rethinksurvival.com/kindle-books/smartphone-survival-apps-book/
- Link 72: https://rethinksurvival.com/kindle-books/survival-uses-book/
- Link 73: https://rethinksurvival.com/kindle-books/get-home-bag-book/
- Link 74:
  https://rethinksurvival.com/books/new-survival-books.php

- Link 75: https://rethinksurvival.com/kindle-books/home-security-book-v2/
- Link 76: https://rethinksurvival.com/books/women-safety-review.php

52868453R00068